Supervising Difficult Employees

Hal Wood

PROVANT MEDIA

4601 121ST Street • Urbandale, Iowa 50323
1-888-776-8268 • fax 515-327-2555
www.provantmedia.com

Supervising Difficult Employees

Hal Wood
Copyright © 1998 by American Media, Inc.

This publication is designed to provide accurate and authoritative information in regard to the subject matter covered. It is sold with the understanding that neither the author nor the publisher is engaged in rendering legal, accounting, or other professional service. If legal advice or other expert assistance is required, the services of a competent professional should be sought.

Credits:
American Media Publishing: Art Bauer
                               Todd McDonald
Editor in Chief: Karen Massetti Miller
Designer: Michelle Glass
Cover Design: Maura Rombalski

Published by American Media, Inc.
4900 University Avenue
West Des Moines, IA 50266-6769

Library of Congress Catalog Card Number 98-73542
Wood, Hal
Supervising Difficult Employees

ISBN 1-884926-96-7

Printed in the United States of America
01 00 99 98   9 8 7 6 5 4 3 2 1

Introduction

When did you encounter your first difficult person in the workplace? Most of us have dealt with at least one on our very first job, and we've seen an endless variety ever since.

When difficult people were your coworkers, you could just ignore them or avoid them as much as possible. But then came that promotion to supervisor, and you were presented with your very own set of difficult employees. No more avoiding or ignoring—you're responsible for them now! The productivity of your area and your staff's morale depend on how you handle these people. Did they tell you about this before you accepted the promotion?

Most supervisors and managers work their way up through the ranks by demonstrating a mastery of skills related to their occupation. After being promoted into management, few new supervisors get the training they need in the "soft" skills of employee relations. The assumption is that if they can do the work that well, they can get others to do the same, and that's a poor assumption.

This book will help you develop the relational skills needed to analyze and cope with a worker displaying difficult behavior. Even if you have an M.B.A., you probably didn't have any courses that dealt with this subject. This book should be used as a resource, not a one-read quick fix. So take a deep sigh, open that objective mind of yours, and go to the following pages for the help you need.

About the Author

Hal Wood developed his people skills while growing up in a rural Missouri town where all the residents knew each other and most of them were related. Adding education to that rich upbringing has enabled Hal to have a successful business management career spanning almost 30 years. His management experience includes the fields of health care, international trade, construction, real estate development, and human resources.

For the past 20 years, Hal has managed his own consulting firm, Advisory Management Services, Inc., in Kansas City, Missouri. During that time, he has personally conducted more than 1,800 training sessions and consulted with hundreds of clients ranging from start-ups to Fortune 500 companies. Hal is a certified member of the Institute of Management Consultants and is active in the Human Resources Management Association and the International Society of Performance Improvement. He also teaches graduate courses in health services management and human resources.

Self-Assessment

Read over the following questions and circle Yes or No depending on how you typically respond to the situations described.

1. I realize that there are personality types that are different from my own.   Yes   No

2. I realize that some personality traits are based in heredity and others are based in environment.   Yes   No

3. I try to adjust my communication style to the style of the person to whom I am speaking.   Yes   No

4. When someone behaves in a way that I find difficult to deal with, I do not regard the individual as a bad person. Instead, I focus on dealing with the behavior.   Yes   No

5. When someone behaves in a way that I find difficult, I look at my own behavior to see if I can relate to that person more effectively.   Yes   No

6. I am aware of my own difficult behaviors and work to correct them.   Yes   No

7. I take time to get to know the employees I supervise and identify their personality traits.   Yes   No

8. As much as possible, I try to give employees I supervise work assignments that are appropriate to their personalities and temperaments.   Yes   No

9. If an employee has an apparent mental health or substance abuse problem, I refer that person to a counselor rather than trying to counsel the person myself.   Yes   No

10. I am familiar with and willing to use my organization's discipline and termination procedures.   Yes   No

Scoring for Self-Assessment

To determine your score, give yourself 10 points for every Yes that you marked and 0 points for each No.

- If you scored 100 or 90 points, you have excellent skills for dealing with the difficult people in your life. Use this book to gain new insights and polish your skills.

- If you scored 80 points, you have some good skills for dealing with difficult people. Use this book to develop those skills further.

- If you scored 70 points, you may not be dealing with difficult people as effectively as you could. Use this book to identify those areas in which you could use improvement.

- If you scored 60 points, you may be having problems dealing with difficult people. Use this book to identify those areas in which you could use improvement.

Chapter *One*

Why Are Some People Difficult to Supervise?

Chapter Objectives

▶   Identify common difficult behaviors.

▶   Explain how people become difficult.

▶   Recognize the supervisor's influence on the worker.

Carmen hated her weekly meetings with Jeff. Every time she gave him another work assignment, he moaned and complained as though everything she asked him to do was completely unreasonable. His workload wasn't any heavier than anyone else's. Why couldn't he just accept his assignments and do his job?

When we're polite, we call them "difficult people." We call them lots of other things too: jerks, weirdos, kooks, screwups, pains in various places, hotheads, strange dudes, loners, rebels, complainers, and just plain rude are some of the printable terms overheard in the workplace. They come in all shapes, sizes, sexes, colors, and ages. After a recent encounter with a young employee, one frustrated supervisor wondered, "How can someone get that messed up in such a short life?"

> Whatever you call those employees you find difficult to supervise, you still need to develop effective ways to work with them.

Whatever you call those employees you find difficult to supervise, you still need to develop effective ways to work with them. This book will help you do that by providing you with insight into what makes employees difficult and helping you develop strategies for coping with them.

What Makes an Employee Difficult?

The term *difficult people* may be a little misleading. People themselves aren't difficult, but their behavior can be. Over the course of our lives, many of us develop behaviors that make it difficult for other people to work with us. Some of these behaviors may simply be irritating while others are actually destructive.

1

Take a Moment

Think about the employees you supervise or manage. Describe the difficult behaviors they are currently demonstrating as well as other difficult behaviors you have observed in the recent past.

_____

_____

_____

_____

_____

_____

What types of behaviors did you list in the exercise above? Compare your list with a list of what other supervisors and managers have observed.

Top 24 Most Difficult Behaviors

1. Dishonesty
2. Incompetence
3. Resistance to change
4. Unresponsiveness
5. Lacking intelligence
6. Treating others unfairly
7. Inflexibility
8. Untruthfulness
9. Lacking imagination
10. Undependability
11. Self-centeredness
12. Avoiding risk
13. Apathy
14. Uncooperativeness
15. Immaturity
16. Laziness
17. Lacking initiative
18. Hostility
19. Disrespectfulness
20. Dependency
21. Negativity or Bitterness
22. Disorganization
23. Jealousy
24. Antisocial behavior

Based on responses of 2,615 managers in research on superior leaders by James Kouzes and Barry Posher at Santa Clara University, 1986. Verified by polls conducted by the author at nationwide seminars.

What Are the Causes of Difficult Behavior?

As a manager or supervisor, you will be able to respond more effectively to difficult behaviors if you understand how they originate. We can identify two primary sources for difficult behavior:

◆ Hereditary characteristics

◆ Formative life experiences

Heredity and experience are the roots of the human personality.

As you might have guessed, heredity and experience are also the sources of normal human behavior; in fact, they are the roots of the human personality.

In the following chapters, we'll consider how heredity and experience work together to create the personality and difficult behaviors, but before we begin, a word of caution: As you read, avoid the temptation to psychoanalyze your employees. Your role is not to serve as a therapist to your employees, but to understand the reasons for their behavior so that you can react appropriately.

Chapter Summary

Over the course of our lives, many of us develop behaviors that may make it difficult for people to work with us. Some of these behaviors may simply be irritating while others are actually destructive.

1

Difficult behaviors are the result of:

◆ Hereditary characteristics

◆ Formative life experiences

In the following chapters, we'll look at ways to identify alternatives for the difficult behaviors you see and appropriate actions to allow the worker to become a productive asset to your workforce.

Self-Check: Chapter One Review

Answers to these questions appear on page 108.

1. People aren't difficult, but their _____ can be.

2. List three of the Top 24 Most Difficult Behaviors.

   a. _____

   b. _____

   c. _____

3. True or False?
   Whether or not people develop difficult behaviors is determined by heredity; their experiences have little to do with it.

Notes

1

Chapter *Two*

Identifying the Sources of Difficult Behavior

Chapter Objectives

▶ Identify hereditary physical, mental, and emotional characteristics that can create difficult behaviors.

▶ Respond appropriately to difficult behaviors whose hereditary sources cannot be altered.

▶ Recognize the four stages of human development and how experiences at each stage may affect behavior.

"But Mom, I want to go out and play now!" Timmy yelled as he paced back and forth in front of the back door.

"No, Timmy, you can't go out now," Marilyn answered. "Dinner will be ready in 10 minutes. Go upstairs and wash your hands and face."

"But I don't want to have dinner now. I want to go out and play!" Timmy whined. "Why do we have to have dinner now, anyway?"

"Because I'm the Mommy and I said so, that's why!" Marilyn responded as she shooed Timmy upstairs. When he was gone, she paused and shook her head in disbelief. "Good grief," she said to herself. "I'm starting to sound more like my mother every day."

Each of us comes into this world with a standard equipment package. The genes a baby inherits at conception help determine the behavior that adult will exhibit in the workplace. Each of us also goes through a variety of life experiences, and the lessons we learn from those experiences also affect our behavior in the workplace. In this chapter, we will consider some of the ways in which heredity and life experience can help create difficult workplace behavior.

2

Heredity as a Source of Difficult Behavior

Hereditary factors influence the three following areas of development:

◆ Physical characteristics

◆ Mental characteristics

◆ Emotional characteristics

In turn, each of these areas of development influence the way people behave both in and out of the workplace.

> The genes a baby inherits at conception help determine the behavior that adult will exhibit in the workplace.

Physical Characteristics and Difficult Behavior

People today are painfully aware of and concerned about their physical characteristics. Television and print media constantly put before us examples of physical perfection. People strive to look like these models and often find that their biggest barrier is their own gene pool. Whether people take after their parents or grandparents, such things as height, weight, hair color, eye color, bone structure, skin tone, hormonal and chemical levels, muscular response, and coordination are firmly established and resist modification.

What does this have to do with difficult behavior we see in later life? Right or wrong, physical appearance is a major determinant of the first impressions people form of us. Although appearance may have nothing to do with a person's nature or talents, research shows that it is the basis of how people are treated by others, especially in the early stages of a relationship.

Even among small children, physical appearance becomes a factor in how relationships develop. It may be the basis for teasing or name-calling and may actually make the difference between acceptance or rejection by others.

For example, studies show that people who are handsome, tall, or well proportioned or who have nice hair have a better chance of being hired for a job than others when work qualifications are otherwise equal.

When our physical characteristics help us to be easily accepted and reinforce a positive self-image, we are more likely to relate positively to other people.

When our physical characteristics help us to be easily accepted and reinforce a positive self-image, we are more likely to relate positively to other people. When our physical characteristics go against model norms, create personal dissatisfaction, and result in frequent rejection, we are more likely to relate negatively to other people and be protective of our own feelings. Resulting negative behaviors could include isolation, introversion, lack of confidence, suspicion, lack of personal care, skepticism, pessimism, bitterness, anger, and hostility. When taken to extremes, these behaviors may require treatment by mental health professionals.

Take a Moment

"Sticks and stones may break my bones, but words will never hurt me." Could this old children's retort be a defense mechanism to cover up how badly the words really did hurt? Were you ever teased about or even given nicknames for a physical characteristic? How did it affect your feelings for and responses to the name caller?

_____

_____

Are any of your staff or coworkers currently experiencing ridicule in the plant or office because of a physical characteristic? Describe the situation.

_____

_____

What should a supervisor do to set the example for the treatment of others based on physical traits?

_____

_____

_____

A supervisor can't do much about a person's physical attributes, so what's the proper response to the last question in the previous exercise? As much as possible, ignore the physical characteristics of your employees and focus on their skills and workplace behavior. There are helpful tips in coming chapters to show you how to do this effectively. Certainly you would not participate in or tolerate behavior that demeans an employee for any reason.

Could negative comments about a person's appearance lead to legal action, such as charges of discrimination? Under antidiscrimination laws, the majority of protected classes are based on visible physical traits. These include age, sex, race, national origin, and disability.

As much as possible, ignore the physical characteristics of your employees and focus on their skills and workplace behavior.

Although sexual harassment is frequently discussed, few realize that illegal harassment can be and has been charged under all areas of protected classes. Any unequal treatment or adverse impact involving these characteristics constitutes illegal discrimination and becomes a risk of legal action against the organization.

Mental Characteristics and Difficult Behavior

Intelligence

What educators measure as I.Q. (Intelligence Quotient) is a hereditary factor with both physical and mental components. How effectively sensory nerves perceive and send signals to the brain for processing, storage, and retrieval affects intelligence levels. Other factors are chemical reactions at the nerve synapses and in the brain. The effectiveness of this miraculous electronic system is determined by the genes and is limited in the amount that it can change.

> **Supervisors can help employees apply their intelligence effectively.**

Supervisors can do little to affect their employees' intelligence levels; however, they can affect how that intelligence is applied to work. Supervisors can help employees apply their intelligence effectively by providing them with specialized instruction, on-the-job training, routine coaching, and team development.

Brain Dominance

As a child develops before and after birth, hormonal levels affect which side of the brain will be dominant. Although most people use both sides of the brain in a balanced way, research suggests that the majority of men have a slight tendency to favor the left side of the brain, and the majority of women have a slight tendency to favor the right side. Therefore, what we often perceive as differences between men and women are really differences caused by brain dominance. Some of the different capabilities that result are listed in the table that follows. As you read it, remember, the information in this area is based on *tendencies*, not *absolutes*.

Left Brain Functions	Right Brain Functions
Facts—storage and retrieval	Emotions—storage and retrieval
Abstract concepts	Physical-environment perception
Math & science	Language, humanities, & history
Processes & systems	Creativity & artistic expression

2

If some of these functions become unbalanced, they can cause difficult behaviors. For example, a left-brained person acting only on facts and logic can be mechanical and insensitive, and can hurt others' feelings. On the other hand, a right-brained person acting on emotional reactions may easily be misled or manipulated into some costly error. The abstract left-brained person can process directions and instructions more easily, especially where maps or symbols are involved. Right-brained people prefer to give and take physical directions by using landmarks. A right-brained person may also be very sensitive to environmental factors and sensory input, such as heat, light, noise, smells, etc.

Left-brained people enjoy the logic of a process or system but may have trouble thinking outside of the box. Right-brained people are creatively looking for different ways to do things and may not conform to policies and procedures well.

Therefore, supervisors need to be alert to the way they coach, teach, and give instructions to ensure that all workers understand. Speak to both sides of the brain by giving examples, allowing input, and asking for questions. When explaining a situation, address the emotional elements involved as well as the facts and logic.

Supervisors need to be alert to the way they coach, teach, and give instructions to ensure that all workers understand.

Take a Moment

Can you think of an employee who seems to favor right-brain processing over left-brain? How about left-brain processing over right? List any difficult behaviors you've noticed below.

Prefers Left-Brain Processing   Prefers Right-Brain Processing

_____   _____

_____   _____

_____   _____

_____   _____

Learning Styles

Heredity also determines the way in which we process input and information: in other words, the way we learn. The three basic learning styles are:

◆ Visual

◆ Auditory

◆ Emotional

Visual learners store information by what they see. This is why visual aids are so important in presentations or training. Visual learners find studying a diagram or reading directions more effective than listening to verbal instructions.

On the other hand, *auditory learners* would rather be told what to do or listen to some type of media to receive information. We've all seen this person trying to learn to use a computer. "I can't understand the manual; just tell me what buttons to hit," is a frequent comment.

Visual learners store information by what they see. *Auditory learners* would rather listen to some type of media to receive information.

The *emotional learner* retains and retrieves information in relation to feelings or reactions. They reinforce their learning by actions and application. "Okay, I've seen or heard what you want me to do, now let me try it," would be a typical response. For this type, on-the-job training and application are critical.

To prevent confusion and misdirected effort, good supervisors will combine visual, verbal, and emotional methods in their instructions and follow-up. If you have a staff member who "doesn't listen," seems "preoccupied," or otherwise responds poorly, try presenting information in a variety of ways, as in the following example.

Example: "Good morning, team! As I describe (auditory) our next project to you, please follow along with the handout (visual) I gave you. Mistakes in application related to this project can result in significant financial losses to the company (emotional)."

The *emotional learner* retains and retrieves information in relation to feelings or reactions.

2

What Were You Doing When . . . ?

To better understand someone's learning style, ask the person to describe what they were doing when they learned of a memorable or historic event, such as the Kennedy assassination or the Oklahoma City bombing. Which senses do they use? "I remember seeing . . ." "The news commentator said . . ." or "I was in shock and felt . . ." The brain retrieves and shares information the same way it was stored by the learning style.

Take a Moment

What learning style do you prefer?

_____

Is this the style you generally use when communicating with your employees? How can you adapt information so that it will be understood by employees with a different learning style?

_____

_____

Mental Illness

Heredity can also be the source of mental disorders based in physiology. Hormonal and blood chemistry imbalances or enzymatic malfunction can lead to serious difficult behaviors. Some of those behaviors can be rooted in bipolar diseases, such as passive-aggressive, manic-depressive, paranoia, and schizophrenia (see next page). Other behaviors, such as extreme hostility, addiction, depression, hyperactivity, attention deficit disorders, and any other mental conditions commonly treated with medication, usually fall into this category.

Heredity can also be the source of mental disorders based in physiology.

Common Mental Health Problems

Anxiety: A feeling of fear or dread caused by internal subjective stimuli that the person may not be able to identify.

Bipolar Disorder: Exhibiting two extreme moods such as manic (high activity, frantic) then depressive (low activity, lethargic).

Compulsion: Intense impulses and urges to follow a pattern, ritual, or behavior (such as having to walk all the way around a car before getting in).

Depression: Feeling dejected, sad, pessimistic, apathetic, and/or hopeless; no interest in people; poor self-image.

Manic: A state of euphoria; excitement and agitation that result in irrationality and the inability to focus attention.

Obsession: A recurring behavior that is contrary to one's own will. Usually seen as an irrational cause and effect relationship, such a "stepping on a crack brings bad luck."

Paranoia: Irrational belief that a number of people and/or things may harm them.

Panic and Phobias: Irrational fears that cause behavioral and physical reactions, such as breathlessness and sweating. Examples include being in close environments, flying in airplanes, and standing in vast open spaces.

Schizophrenia: Impaired ability to be logical or rational. May include delusions, visions, and the inability to relate to reality.

2

Mental illness is more common than you might think—researchers estimate that one in five people has a diagnosable mental health problem. What should you, as a supervisor, do when an employee's behavior leads you to suspect he or she has a mental illness? Don't play psychiatrist! Refer the person to competent health professionals. If your company has an employee assistance program, it can help the employee identify the root of the problem behavior and begin treatment without stigma or violation of privacy. If you don't have such a program, gently and kindly ask the person to seek professional help, and have a referral ready.

Take a Moment

How could you help an employee who you suspect has a mental health problem? Are you familiar with any employee assistance programs your company might offer? If not, check with your Human Resources or Personnel Department so that you'll have information available in case you ever have to make a referral.

Emotional Characteristics and Difficult Behavior

■ Some view the cup as half empty; others view the cup as half full.

Different people can have very different reactions to the same set of circumstances.

As the old saying above illustrates, different people can have very different reactions to the same set of circumstances. The way you are affected by what goes on around you, how you express yourself, and how you relate to others are all in part established by heredity. We've all heard comments about children like, "She's acting just like her mother," or "His father does that too."

These hereditary emotional characteristics are at the core of what we refer to as the "personality." We'll consider how personalities are shaped in the following chapter. But first, we'll consider a second source of difficult behavior—life experience.

Experience as a Source of Difficult Behavior

■ When Gwyneth looked at Dominick's proposal, she couldn't believe her eyes. Dominick had taken Gwyneth's ideas and presented them as his own. Gwyneth had shared her ideas with Dominick to get his feedback before writing her own proposal. They'd always worked so well together, she never dreamed he'd steal them. "That's the last time I'll ever trust a coworker," she muttered to herself as she threw the proposal into the wastebasket.

2

We've seen how heredity can be the source of a number of the difficult behaviors supervisors encounter in the workplace. But heredity isn't the only source for these behaviors. People adjust their behaviors based on the experiences they encounter throughout their lives. Most research indicates that the basis of the behavior of a normal adult is about 50 percent heredity and 50 percent experience.

> **People adjust their behaviors based on the experiences they encounter throughout their lives.**

Experiences teach us to modify our behaviors through both positive and negative reinforcement. If we take an action that leads to a positive result, we are likely to repeat that action. If we take an action that leads to a negative result, we are likely to avoid repeating that action.

Sometimes we adopt difficult behaviors because they help us achieve the results we want. For example, children who get what they want through temper tantrums can become adults who get what they want through emotional outbursts.

We may also adopt difficult behaviors when they help us avoid something unpleasant. For example, children who are criticized or belittled for expressing themselves may become adults who avoid sharing their expertise or insight even when that information could benefit their work teams.

Take a Moment

Everyone can look back on his or her life and find defining moments that still affect him or her today, both positively and negatively. Maybe you won a spelling bee or made a game-winning shot. Maybe a teacher embarrassed you in front of the class, or you experienced a traumatic injury or illness. Identify three such situations from your life and consider how they currently affect you.

Situation   Effect

1. _____   _____

   _____   _____

2. _____   _____

   _____   _____

3. _____   _____

   _____   _____

Human beings all pass through a series of developmental stages in which certain formative experiences can have a major impact. Many difficult behaviors found in adults can be traced to experiences in one of the following developmental stages.

Early Childhood (Preschool)

How children are treated during early childhood determines a lot of their coping mechanisms.

How children are treated during early childhood determines a lot of their coping mechanisms. Most fears are developed in early childhood. Children are born with only two fears: fear of loud noises and fear of falling. Children develop other fears based on their experiences. Are they loved and cuddled, or are they isolated, roughly handled, or physically or mentally abused? Are they encouraged and rewarded, or are they ridiculed and punished? Children learn from experience even at this young age and can develop difficult behaviors that will remain with them throughout adulthood.

Late Childhood (Elementary School)
This is the stage where self-focus diminishes and relating to others begins to take precedence. Children become more aware of their parents' behavior and influence. For example, did the family stay together, and if not, did the child feel guilty or responsible? Did either or both parents become passive in relating to the child? How was discipline handled? What did parents say about work and their jobs? Did the child resent a parent's job for taking too much of the parent's time?

2

This is also the stage at which children learn how to develop relationships with their own age group at school. How did they respond to the authority figure of the teacher? Did they make friends easily? Were they teased, embarrassed, picked on by bullies? All of these situations are registered in the child's memory.

> In late childhood, children become more aware of their parents' behavior and influence.

■ Jake's father had high standards and didn't like mistakes. In fact, when Jake's mistakes as a young child were discovered, he knew what was coming—"You just don't seem to be able to do anything right. You'll probably never amount to anything!" Jake heard that so often, he began to believe it. If he couldn't get his father's attention by what he did right, he decided to excel at what he did wrong, so Jake ended up in reform school at age 14.

The negative tape continued to play as Jake entered the workplace. Sometimes Jake's boss sounded just like his father, and Jake's relationships with coworkers were strained because Jake had developed an aggressive and sarcastic manner to hide his insecurities. Even though his work skills and effort were good, he just didn't fit in. He frequently changed jobs, both voluntarily and involuntarily.

Even into his late thirties, Jake was still haunted by his father's favorite phrase. He finally decided to seek psychological counseling and was able to resolve a great deal of his feelings toward his father. Rebellion against authority and the inability to relate to coworkers led Jake to a brilliant alternative. He would avoid them by starting his own business.

Today Jake is a successful business owner. He still struggles with his difficult behavior in relating to friends and employees, but he's getting better with practice. He's one of the lucky ones.

Adolescence (Ages 12–16)

At about age 12, children enter a two- to four-year period of emotional swings and irrationality due to hormonal development. They emerge with adult equipment and a mind that still wants to go out and play. Children develop coping mechanisms and self-awareness by working through this confusion. Comparisons with perfection may cause eating disorders. Parents suddenly find that most of their ability to influence their child is gone, and the adolescent's attention now turns to the peer group for acceptance.

The effects of choosing the right friends or falling in with the "wrong crowd" will have a marked effect on a child's development.

Early Adulthood (Ages 17–23)

A key challenge for young people at this age is learning how to handle responsibility. How much freedom are they given to make their own decisions? How do they handle such challenges as driving a car, exposure to illegal substances, and relating to the opposite sex?

This is the age when most young adults are introduced to the workplace for the first time. Did they like their work? How were they treated by others, especially older adults? In polls, almost everyone vividly remembers his or her first boss. Do you? Are your memories positive or negative, and how has that initial experience affected your work and the way you supervise?

> At about age 12, children enter a two- to four-year period of emotional swings and irrationality due to hormonal development.

> A key challenge of early adulthood is learning to handle responsibility.

Take a Moment

Has it occurred to you yet that you may be someone's first boss? Think about how you come across to that impressionable young worker. List some behaviors in the categories below that could improve that first experience and that person's lifelong memory of you:

Things to start doing:

_____

_____

Things to stop doing:

_____

_____

Things to continue doing:

_____

_____

Each employee's experiences during these developmental stages determine what you get in a pool of job applicants or the group of employees you inherit when you're promoted. You may dream of hiring well-balanced, energetic employees who communicate well, learn quickly, get along with everyone, and are eager to excel. But in reality, you may be working with employees whose work is affected by poor self-image, guilt, the pain of multiple rejections, money problems, or the inability to relate to others. Mentally, they could be in need of professional counseling. Addiction, depression, bipolar mood swings, eating disorders, and violent behavior are common in today's workplace. Educationally, reading, writing, and basic math skills may be minimal or absent.

> **Each employee's experiences during these developmental stages determine what you get in a pool of job applicants.**

Chapter Summary

Many of the difficult behaviors observed in the workplace originate from a person's heredity. Hereditary factors influence three major areas of development:

◆ Physical characteristics

◆ Mental characteristics

◆ Emotional characteristics

Many people form their first impressions of us based on our physical appearance. When our physical characteristics help us to be easily accepted and reinforce a positive self-image, we are more likely to relate positively to other people. But when our physical characteristics bring us rejection and personal dissatisfaction, we are more likely to relate negatively to people and exhibit negative behaviors.

Our behavior is also influenced by mental characteristics, including intelligence, brain dominance, and learning styles. Supervisors and managers cannot change these mental characteristics, but they can adjust the way they relate to employees so that they communicate effectively with a variety of people. At their most extreme, mental characteristics may include mental illness. When managers or supervisors suspect that an employee's behavior is the result of mental illness, they should refer that employee to a mental health professional.

The way we are affected by what goes on around us and the ways we express ourselves and relate to others are influenced by our emotional characteristics. These hereditary emotional characteristics form the core of what we refer to as the personality. We will learn more about the personality and its effect on behavior in upcoming chapters.

When confronted with difficult behavior, a supervisor or manager needs to consider the employee's physical, mental, and emotional makeup. By understanding these sources of the behavior, the manager or supervisor may be able to improve the situation by changing the way he or she relates to the employee.

Self-Check: Chapter Two Review

Answers to these questions appear on page 108.

1. Hereditary factors influence these three areas of development:

   a. _____

   b. _____

   c. _____

2. How does our physical appearance influence our behavior?

   _____

   _____

3. The three basic learning styles are:

   a. _____

   b. _____

   c. _____

4. True or False?
   If a supervisor believes that an employee's difficult behaviors are rooted in mental illness, that supervisor has a responsibility to counsel the employee personally.

5. List the four stages of development described in this chapter and the major developmental change associated with each.

   a. _____ _____

   b. _____ _____

   c. _____ _____

   d. _____ _____

Chapter *Three*

Recognizing the Role of Personality

Chapter Objectives

▶ Explain the relationship between heredity, experience, and personality.

▶ Identify the four basic personality types and their primary traits.

▶ Explain how personality traits can create difficult behavior.

▶ Recognize the type of influence a supervisor can have in creating behavioral change.

Dante watched as Rebecca led the new work team's first meeting. He hadn't known her for long, but he could already recognize some of her behaviors. She was animated and expressive as she led the group, yet kept everyone on the task at hand and continually emphasized the results they were to achieve. "Yes," Dante thought to himself, "I've seen her type before."

> **Heredity and experience aren't just the sources of *difficult* behavior; they are also the sources of *normal* behavior.**

We've seen how heredity and experience can both be the sources of the difficult behavior we encounter in the workplace. But as we mentioned previously, heredity and experience aren't just the sources of *difficult* behavior; they are also the sources of *normal* behavior—and of the personality itself. Graphically, we can represent the relationship in this way:

Heredity + Experience = Personality

As our opening example suggests, some people share similar personality traits that are demonstrated through their behavior. If you think of the people you know, you can probably identify several who are expressive and outgoing as well as others who are shy and retiring. You might know some who react quickly and impetuously as well as others who take their time and proceed cautiously.

Shared traits like these allow us to group people into basic personality types. None of these personality types is inherently difficult; however, difficult behavior can occur when normal personality traits are developed to the point of dysfunctionality. That is why one of the best ways to understand and cope with difficult behavior is to recognize the different personality types one can encounter in the workplace and ways in which each can become dysfunctional.

> **Some people share similar personality traits that are demonstrated through their behavior.**

3

Take a Moment

Do you know any people who seem to share similar personality traits? List a key trait and the names of some people who share it below.

Trait: _____

Shared by: _____

_____

_____

What Are the Personality Types?

Insight into personality types is nothing new. In ancient Greece (about 2000 B.C.), Hippocrates had tremendous observational powers. He documented that people tend to behave in four basic styles or "humors."

After many years of psychological research, we have improved very little on the accuracy of Hippocrates' original observations. Today, there are well over 40 different personality instruments designed to identify a person's dominant personality type and how all four types may blend together. Some are self-scoring, some are scored by the organization representing the instrument, and some are computer-generated on-site by software. Instruments may vary in terminology, but what they identify are the same four basic types that Hippocrates observed and that supervisors see in the workplace on a daily basis.

You've probably noticed that we've avoided referring to the four personality types by name. That's because the names vary depending on what profile instrument you read. Most instruments apply their own names to the four types to avoid copyright violations. Some use colors or names of animals that demonstrate key behaviors. But no matter what you call them, they're the same four styles.

Heartwise Communications uses four terms in their computer-generated personality instrument that accurately describe the four types:

◆ Dominant

◆ Extrovert

◆ Patient

◆ Conformist

We will use these terms throughout the rest of this book.* Each style will be individually defined and discussed in its own chapter, but for now, here are some initial definitions and comparisons.

* Terms used by permission of Heartwise Communications. For further information call 816/765-9611 or write 9600 E. 129th St. #B, Kansas City, MO 64149.

We can begin to look at the four types by identifying the similarities between Dominants and Extroverts and contrasting them to Patients and Conformists.

3

Dominants & Extroverts	Patients & Conformists
1. Take a general, big-picture approach (see forests)	1. Pay attention to detail in their surroundings (see knotholes)
2. Communicate in paragraphs of thought (may not say what they're actually thinking)	2. Communicate specific words in context (say exactly what they are thinking)
3. Expressive and outgoing	3. Good listeners and introverted
4. Starters	4. Finishers
5. Multiple-task-oriented (does 6–10 things at once)	5. One activity at a time, done well, without interruption
6. Task- and results-oriented	6. Process-oriented
7. Flexible and loosely structured	7. Prefer structure and guidelines
8. Impetuous and reactive	8. Cautious and thoughtful

In spite of their similarities, even the traits that are grouped together are unique in some of the following ways:

Dominants	Extroverts
Very task-oriented and driven	More people-oriented and laid-back
Make factual and logical decisions	Make emotional decisions (gullible)
Rely on individual effort	Rely on team and group effort
Intense and assertive	Happy-go-lucky and congenial

Patients	Conformists
Need substantial contact	Content to be alone
Generally resist change	Change readily if facts support it
Good at mediating conflict	Decide based on facts and principles
Take action for causes	Support causes passively

Personal Note: When I was first exposed to information about personality styles, I was more than 30 years old. The more I learned about this 4,000-year-old body of knowledge, the more upset I became that no one had taught me about it sooner, not even as a part of a graduate education. I use this information several times a day, in both business and personal situations. It is amazing to me that it is not a part of our secondary educational system, nor is it general knowledge to most of my clients and customers. As it is discussed, please consider all of the possible applications to your personal and business life.

Take a Moment

Based on the descriptions of the four personality types, can you identify your own type? Write it in the space below.

_____

Now, think of an employee whose behavior you find difficult. Can you identify that person's personality type? Write it in the space below.

_____

Now compare the two personality types. Which of the other person's traits do you find most difficult to deal with?

_____

_____

_____

Which of your traits do you think the other person has the most difficulty dealing with?

_____

_____

_____

3

Universality of the Personality Types

Amazingly, the observations Hippocrates made about human nature in Greece 4,000 years ago are still accurate today. People's behaviors may be somewhat modified by their cultures, but the basic personality types are still very identifiable. Personality profiles have been conducted in many foreign countries with no major variance in the presence of the traits. You may find it reassuring to work with practical and useful information that is consistent across many different cultures over a long period of time.

We see a lot of emphasis today on recognizing cultural diversity. We should strive to understand different cultures so that we do not offend others, but the emphasis of much of the training in this area seems to be on how we're different. The beauty of relating to people based on personality type is that everybody has one! Once we understand people's personalities enough to relate on that basis, their physical appearance or background shouldn't affect our behavior toward them that much. In other words, the basis of prejudice is greatly diminished.

Observing the Types in Action

> Each person has some unique blend of all four personality types, with one type being prevalent.

So how do the four personality types work? Every person has some unique blend of all four types. One type is usually prevalent, but that prevalence can shift as a person adapts to situations and environments. For example, many people find themselves in jobs that require skills and behaviors different from their naturally prevalent type. They may adopt a secondary personality style in the workplace, but in other settings, their prevalent personality will resurface. If these differences are extreme, work may become stressful, and difficult behaviors may develop.

As you identify the personality types of employees in the workplace, remember that any attempt to analyze or predict behavior is based only on the tendencies of that personality type. There are no absolutes in the areas of personality-based behavior because the variety of combinations is infinite.

Valuing All Personality Types

As you begin to recognize the personality types, remember that each is a variation of normal human behavior and valuable in its own way. For example, any personality type can produce a leader, but leaders with different personality types won't lead in the same way. Likewise, people of each personality type can be successful, but they won't achieve success in the same way.

In the workplace, outcomes tend to be more successful when a blending of personality traits is present. If all the members of a team or work group were the same, they would simply duplicate each other's strengths and vulnerabilities. They wouldn't have much conflict, but needed skills would be missing. If a blend of the traits is present, some friction from the different approaches will occur, but the resulting efforts will be better balanced in their planning and execution.

Just as each personality type has the potential to succeed, each has the potential to generate difficult behavior. What we identify as difficult behavior is simply the negative or undesirable side of one of the four. There may be hundreds of difficult behaviors, but they all come from the same four personality types that generate positive behaviors. If we can understand the four basic types and how to respond to them, we have a very good chance of either preventing or managing their difficult behavior.

Just as each personality type has the potential to succeed, each has the potential to generate difficult behavior.

3

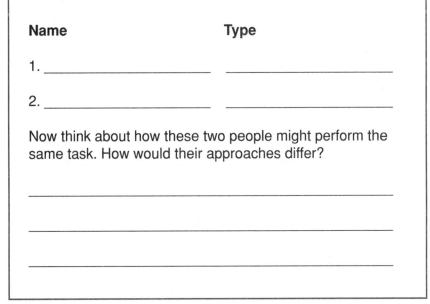

Take a Moment

Think of two people you know with different personality types. Write their names and personality types in the spaces below.

Name   **Type**

1. _____   _____

2. _____   _____

Now think about how these two people might perform the same task. How would their approaches differ?

_____

_____

_____

Encouraging Behavioral Change

Before we consider the four personality types in greater detail, let's identify some basic traits all people share that can provide us with insight into managing difficult behavior:

1. **People view situations from their own perspective.**
   When people are confronted with a problem, their first reaction is usually, "How will this affect me?" Putting the interests of others ahead of your own is commendable, but when the chips are down, most of us revert to self-interest. Self-preservation efforts can generate a number of difficult behaviors, such as denial, anger, aggressiveness, defensiveness, sabotage, change resistance, jealousy, and withdrawal.

2. **You can't change other people.**
   Just as people generally view situations from their own perspective, they do things for their own reasons—not yours. You cannot make a difficult person change; the person him- or herself must decide to change.

   Some attempts to change difficult behavior resort to the use of fear or punishment. While such tactics may result in short-term behavioral change, underlying attitudes probably won't change, and any behavioral change probably won't be permanent. Once again, the only person who can change a difficult person is the difficult person him- or herself. So what do we do now?

3. **You *can* change environments and your own behavior to motivate others to change themselves.**

   ■ "Oh great! He's the one causing all the problems, and the burden of change falls on me! Why shouldn't he change? I'm the supervisor here."

   It doesn't seem fair, but the logic is inescapable. You want difficult people to change, but you can't force them. They won't change unless they perceive it to be in their best interest. You need to discover what their needs are and how to meet them in a reasonable way. In the following chapters, we'll see how you can use your knowledge of the personality types to provide people with incentives to change their difficult behavior.

> You cannot make a difficult person change; the person him- or herself must decide to change.

Chapter Summary

Heredity and experience are not just the sources of difficult behavior. They are also the sources of normal behavior and the personality itself. Heredity + Experience = Personality.

People share many similar personality traits. These shared traits allow us to group people into basic personality types. In this book, we will refer to the four personality types as:

- ◆ Dominant
- ◆ Extrovert
- ◆ Patient
- ◆ Conformist

3

Each personality type is a variation of normal human behavior and valuable in its own way. What we identify as difficult behavior is simply the negative or undesirable side of one of the four types.

When dealing with difficult behavior, remember that you cannot change other people. People only change when they want to change. You can, however, change environments and your own behavior to motivate others to change themselves.

Self-Check: Chapter Three Review

Answers to the following questions appear on page 109.

1. Complete the following equation:

   _____ + _____ = Personality

2. Match the following personality types with their characteristics:

   _____ Dominant

   _____ Extrovert

   _____ Patient

   _____ Conformist

   a. Good at mediating conflict
   b. Makes decisions based on emotions
   c. Very task-oriented and driven
   d. Content to be alone

3. True or False?
   Each person has a prevalent personality type and never displays traits related to the other types.

4. True or False?
   No personality type is inherently difficult.

5. You can't change other people. You can only change _____ and _____ to motivate others to change themselves.

Notes

Chapter *Four*

Supervising the Dominant Personality

Chapter Objectives

▶ Identify and understand the Dominant type.

▶ Recognize difficult Dominant behavior.

▶ Prevent difficult Dominant behavior, and deal with it effectively when it does occur.

Sally couldn't see why everyone was so concerned about the merger. It would give them more money to work with, which meant that they could finally start some of the projects they'd relegated to the back burner. There was one in particular she'd been wanting to tackle for a year. She made a mental note to talk to her boss about the possibility of serving as team leader for that assignment—she really wanted to see it done right.

Identifying Dominant Traits

About 15 percent of the general population will have their highest score on the Dominant type. Dominants are one of the easiest personality types to identify. Following are some of their basic traits.

◆ Dominants are always aware of goals and tasks, which drive them to accomplishment.

Dominants are always aware of goals and tasks, which drive them to accomplishment.

◆ Dominants are creative and innovative and can even have ideas while they sleep. They have enough ideas to keep several people busy with implementation.

◆ Dominants welcome change because it means progress. They lie awake at night thinking of ways to change things.

- Once Dominants have an idea, they quickly take action, usually in a "follow me" mode. They lead by example to get results.

- When Dominants encounter obstacles, they hit them head on. Dominants seek out challenges, and stress merely heightens their efforts.

- Dominants enjoy risk—no risk, no fun! The Dominant's cycle of activity can be described as: Situation or problem ◗ risk ◗ challenge ◗ effort ◗ accomplishment ◗ satisfaction.

- Dominants feel the need to control people and resources to accomplish a task. They often volunteer for leadership to gain control.

- Dominants are natural problem solvers and decision makers. They are confident, and others often look to them for leadership.

- Dominants are active, fast, and assertive.

- Dominants base their communication on facts and logic.

Frequent Dominant career choices include supervision, sales, trial attorneys, law enforcement, military, coaching, construction, fire fighting, and manufacturing.

Recent Dominant presidents include Harry Truman, Lyndon Johnson, and sometimes Ronald Reagan.

Dominant public figures include former British Prime Minister Margaret Thatcher, General George Patton, Donald Trump, Lee Iacocca, Ross Perot, Hillary Rodham Clinton, and Indiana University basketball coach Bobby Knight.

4

Dominants base their communication on facts and logic.

Take a Moment

List the names of people you know at work and in your personal life who display Dominant traits.

_____

_____

Preventing Dominants from Becoming Difficult

As we saw in the last chapter, the key to improving relationships is to modify *your own* behavior to relate to the other person's personality. Adopting these behaviors can help prevent Dominants from engaging in a difficult response.

What Dominants Like

Ask Dominants for their ideas and input.

◆ Ask for their ideas and input. If they don't participate in the problem solving and/or decision making, they will reject the outcome even when they agree with it.

◆ Show respect for their opinions and judgment as long as you don't compromise your own position. Do not agree just to agree. They will test your convictions and sometimes make absurd statements just to see how you respond.

◆ In verbal and written communication, make your point quickly. They get impatient with long explanations and lead-ins.

◆ Use factual and logical summaries. They don't want details or emotional appeals.

◆ If you mean it, offer your cooperation and support for their approach or project. They will probably delegate some of it to you on the spot.

◆ Be direct and honest with your opinions. They respect courage and willingness to take a stand even if they disagree with you.

- ◆ Don't be afraid to confront issues. They love it!

- ◆ If possible, provide situations involving competition, especially where there are clear winners and losers.

What Dominants Dislike

- ◆ Do not write or speak with too much detail. Take a general bottom-line approach.

- ◆ Do not try to control their actions or responses.

- ◆ Do not be slow or plodding in movement or actions. Wasted time and laziness are unacceptable.

- ◆ Do not become a barrier to progress or accomplishment.

- ◆ Never make excuses or emotional pleas! They hate whining.

- ◆ Do not resist change without providing facts to support your approach.

4

Take a Moment

Choose a Dominant person in the workplace with whom you would like to improve your relationship. (Write that person's initials here: _____)

From the information just discussed, pick two actions that you will take in order to adapt to his or her behavior and write them below:

1._____

2._____

Now select two actions that you will avoid doing in order to adapt to his or her behavior and write them below:

1._____

2._____

Implement your written plan of action on your next encounter and develop plans of action for other Dominant people in your workplace.

Recognizing Typical Dominant Difficult Behaviors

When a dominant person's behavior becomes difficult, the results are often dramatic! The other personality types usually become difficult in response to an undesirable person or situation. Dominant types have been known to become difficult just to get a response or to liven things up if they're bored. They love a spirited debate.

Difficult Behaviors and Recommended Responses

Behaving Insensitively to Others
Behavior:
Dominants' task orientation may create insensitivity to people and feelings. If you're in the way of goal accomplishment, you can get run over. They don't intend to bulldoze over others, and they usually don't know they've done it.

Response:
Confront Dominants about their actions and how they made you feel or the effect they had. Ask them to give more thought to how others will perceive and respond before they speak or take action. When problems are pointed out, they are usually sorry and apologize.

> When problems are pointed out, Dominants are usually sorry and apologize.

4

Desiring Change
Behavior:
The Dominant need for innovation and change can be disruptive to those trying to maintain the status quo.

Response:
Commend Dominants for their progressive approach and ask them if they obtained input and feedback from others before deciding and taking action. If not, request they do so and communicate any plans for change openly.

Needing to Lead
Behavior:
The desire to lead often causes Dominants to ignore established authority. This can be very threatening and disruptive for a supervisor.

Response:
Check your own defensiveness first, then ask them to put themselves in your position and evaluate their own behavior. Ask them how they would feel or respond. Explain how not following proper channels can cause disruption and misunderstanding.

Taking Control
Behavior:
The Dominant's controlling actions can appear defensive and irritate others who desire to lead. Loss of respect may result.

Response:
Confront Dominants and ask them why they need to be in control. If you have the authority, ask them to opt out of leadership so that others can have a turn. Watch for sabotage or undermining.

Creating Explosive Confrontations
Behavior:

> Dominants are the personality type most prone to physically attacking someone.

The Dominant's response to someone generating obstacles is direct confrontation that can become verbally and physically explosive. Red-faced anger with exaggerated gestures is common, much like a baseball coach charging out of the dugout to question an umpire's call. Dominants are the personality type most prone to physically attacking someone.

Response:
Act like an umpire! Don't back up, or they'll keep coming. Don't step forward, or they'll accelerate before impact. Stay as calm as possible and make direct eye contact. Let them blow off steam until they run down. Do not try to gain control of the situation. When they calm down, respond slowly and quietly. They may apologize, and then they will forget almost everything they said in about 15 minutes.

Seeking Risk
Behavior:
The Dominant need for risk and challenge makes the other personalities uncomfortable, anxious, uncertain, and overly cautious.

Response:
Inform Dominants that their actions are upsetting and disruptive to others. State that you do not support what they want to do or that you choose not to participate. Give reasons why as long as they don't sound like excuses.

Making Hasty Decisions
Behavior:

A rapid reaction to problems and decisions without analysis can lead to problems. Dominants can be confidently wrong, and the only way to turn them is to prove the error with facts and provide a better alternative.

Response:

Ask Dominants for facts to back up their position, and ask them to brainstorm additional solutions and other alternatives. They're very creative.

Appearing Impatient
Behavior:

Dominant mannerisms may be imposing. They move fast, make direct eye contact, and often stand with arms folded or hands on hips. They often come across as impatient and in a hurry.

4

Response:

Ask them if they have other demands on their time. Try to get past the body language and concentrate on content. Model the mannerisms you would like to see and they'll pick up on it. Imposing behavior may be used to mask insecurities.

Dominants often come across as impatient and in a hurry.

Communicating Unclearly
Behavior:

The Dominant factual communication style may be perceived as curt and rude. It may also be difficult to understand because Dominants can sometimes present the facts of a case without actually stating their opinion. You may not guess what Dominants are saying or thinking, but they will swear they discussed the issue with you.

Response:

Repeat back to them what you understand and get confirmation.

Seeking Revenge
Behavior:

Dominant people become upset if they think they're being taken advantage of. They can become vengeful and bitter and carry a grudge. They have good memories for bad experiences and will get even if given the chance.

Response:

When working with Dominants, explain what's in it for them. Be fair and objective and point out areas where they need to be cautious, especially financial situations.

Dominants' desire to excel and their ability to innovate and take risks make them valuable employees. Take advantage of these useful positive traits by working to curb negative Dominant behavior before it has a chance to develop.

Take a Moment

Ever since you were transferred from another department to become supervisor of this one, an employee named Dick has seemed out to get you. Openly combative in staff and team meetings, he makes comments that border on mutiny and always has another way to do things. He has deliberately stalled on some of his assignments just to get you to say something to him.

Other team and staff members say that when they work with Dick, he orders them around like he was the boss and has contradicted your advice on some assignments. Others have complained that he has lost his temper and yelled at them when they weren't staying up with his pace.

Reviewing the preceding tips, how would you handle these issues with Dick?

_____

_____

_____

_____

How would you handle the situation in the previous exercise? Here's one approach: First, check to see if Dick applied for your position when it was open. Jealousy could be a factor in his behavior.

Whatever the motivation, Dick's *need to lead* and *taking control* behaviors are undermining your authority. Dominants respect strong leadership, and you will need to confront Dick about his actions. Do this one-on-one, not around other employees. Describe some examples of Dick's negative behaviors and ask him to explain the actions you have observed. Inform him that his job is in jeopardy and insist that any future disagreement be directed to you in the form of a constructive suggestion or solution. Spend more time coaching in Dick's work area to observe compliance.

Chapter Summary

Dominants have many positive qualities that can make them an asset for your team. They are creative, innovative, and driven to succeed. They enjoy risk, seek challenges, and meet obstacles head on.

You can make the most of these Dominant personality traits by asking Dominants for their ideas and input and showing respect for their opinions and judgment. Provide Dominants with opportunities to lead, innovate, and take risks. When communicating with Dominants, make your point quickly, using factual and logical summaries.

When Dominants believe someone is blocking their progress, their behavior can become difficult. If a Dominant becomes confrontational, don't back down, and don't become confrontational yourself. Instead, let them blow off steam, then respond slowly and quietly.

Self-Check: Chapter Four Review

Answers to these questions appear on page 109.

1. Which of the following is *not* a Dominant trait?
   a. Enjoys risk.
   b. Feels the need to be in control.
   c. Slow to take action.
   d. Creative and innovative.

2. True or False?
   If Dominants don't participate in problem solving and/or decision making, they will reject the outcome even when they agree with it.

3. True or False?
   Dominants appreciate communication that includes details and emotional appeals.

4. The Dominant's task orientation may create insensitivity to people and feelings. How can you respond to this difficult behavior?

   _____

   _____

   _____

5. True or False?
   When dealing with Dominants, be direct and honest with your opinions. They respect courage and willingness to take a stand even if they don't agree with you.

Notes

4

Chapter *Five*

Supervising the Extrovert Personality

Chapter Objectives

▶ Identify and understand the Extrovert type.

▶ Recognize difficult Extrovert behavior.

▶ Prevent difficult Extrovert behavior, and deal with it effectively when it does occur.

Paul hated his new job assignment. He was supposed to enter new customer information in the database and then proofread it to be sure there were no errors. He couldn't stand repetitive, detailed work like that. He'd much rather be working with the customers themselves. "Maybe I should talk to the boss," he muttered to himself. "There's got to be something in customer service."

Identifying Extrovert Traits

About 20 percent of the general population will score the highest on the Extrovert type. Because they have a high need for people in their lives, they have learned many ways to avoid being difficult for fear of offending someone.

When confronted with difficult behavior, Extroverts usually respond positively. Some of their normal behaviors follow:

Extroverts are oriented toward people rather than tasks.

◆ Extroverts are oriented toward people rather than tasks. Said another way, they'd rather visit than work.

◆ Extroverts love to meet people. They have good social skills and usually make favorable impressions. They enjoy networking meetings and parties.

◆ Extroverts focus their communication skills on influencing helpful behavior in others. They want you to like what they like. They will recommend things for you to do and try that they believe will help you.

◆ Extroverts have a sincere, compelling desire to help others. They will gladly put themselves out and disrupt their own schedule to assist someone or help that person feel better. If you show appreciation for their efforts, they will watch you to see when you need help again.

◆ Extroverts' emotions run near the surface. Their actions are based much more on feelings than fact.

◆ Extroverts remain optimistic even in difficult situations. They can be ankle deep in horse manure and still be excited about petting the pony. Their trademark is positive, upbeat behavior.

◆ Extroverts crave variety. They hate doing anything the same way twice. As a result, they are very flexible and adaptable to change.

◆ Extroverts enjoy entertaining and love to be the focus of attention. Extroverts are often the class clown in school.

◆ Extroverts overflow with creativity and imagination. This is the child who opens a gift and would rather play with the box than the toy that came in it. The toy is too structured. If you need new approaches to a problem, let them at it.

◆ Extroverts excel in teamwork situations. They like seeing groups of people work together to accomplish something. They will readily sacrifice themselves for the good of the team.

Extroverts focus their communication skills on influencing helpful behavior in others.

5

57

Frequent Extrovert career choices include receptionist, sales, advertising, public relations, entertainment, public speaking, retail, and restaurant positions. They also enjoy work in human resources, communications/broadcasting, politics, and entrepreneurship.

Recent Extrovert presidents include Franklin Roosevelt, Ronald Reagan, and Bill Clinton.

Extrovert public figures include Robin Williams, Red Skelton, Jonathan Winters, most Miss Americas, Oprah Winfrey, Newt Gingrich, Whitney Houston, and Phyllis Diller.

Take a Moment

List the names of people you know at work and in your personal life who display Extrovert traits:

_____

_____

_____

_____

Preventing Extroverts from Becoming Difficult

Based on the above traits, preventing difficult behavior from an Extrovert is really pretty easy. In fact, you would have to try hard to upset this easygoing person who is out to please and help others. The following tips can be used to stabilize and improve relationships with Extroverts.

What Extroverts Like

◆ Act pleasant and personable. Extroverts like to be around others who are "up" and energetic.

◆ Give Extroverts a sincere compliment on some achievement or action. They need a lot of appreciation and affirmation from others, especially when they've been helpful.

Give Extroverts a sincere compliment on some achievement or action.

◆ Ask Extroverts for their opinion, or ask any open question that lets them speak. They will try to dominate the conversation anyway, so make it easy.

◆ Be attentive when Extroverts try to help you. If possible, tell them of some action you intend to take based on their advice.

◆ Put Extroverts in a creative situation in which they have to come up with a variety of alternatives or try something new.

◆ Provide Extroverts with a challenge or a situation with some light competition. They don't have a "kill" or "win" instinct; they just want to have fun. Losing doesn't seem to bother them.

What Extroverts Dislike

◆ Don't make Extroverts compete for attention. Let them have their moment.

◆ Don't assign Extroverts primarily to routine tasks. They hate repetition.

◆ Whenever possible, avoid making Extroverts deal with excessive policies, procedures, rules, and regulations.

◆ Don't ignore Extroverts or direct your attention elsewhere when they're talking.

5

Don't insist that Extroverts get too involved in details.

◆ Avoid assigning Extroverts to solo tasks. They hate being isolated from others.

◆ Don't insist that Extroverts get too involved in details. They like a general, big-picture approach.

◆ Avoid forcing help on Extroverts. They like helping others, so it's hard for them to accept help. You can offer to help, but don't insist if they say "no, thanks."

Take a Moment

Choose an Extrovert person in the workplace with whom you would like to improve your relationship. (Write that person's initials here: _____)

From the information just discussed, pick two actions that you will take in order to adapt to his or her behavior and write them below:

1._____

2._____

Now select two actions that you will avoid doing in order to adapt to his or her behavior and write them below:

1._____

2._____

Implement your written plan of action on your next encounter and develop plans of action for other Extrovert people in your workplace.

Recognizing Typical Extrovert Difficult Behaviors

You may not immediately recognize when an Extrovert is being difficult. They're as covert with their difficult behavior as they are open with their normal behavior. Sometimes they're smiling when in the act. The results of their difficult behavior may not be seen until a later time. Here are some samples and how to respond:

> **You may not immediately recognize when an Extrovert is being difficult.**

Difficult Behaviors and Recommended Responses

Using Others for Support
Behavior:
Extroverts sometimes use other team or work group members for support or to get their way. They live for group approval, and they may rally group pressure to influence decisions.

Response:
Gently try to separate them from the group into a one-on-one situation. They quickly lose their defensiveness and become flexible again. Also, providing open and truthful information to other staff may prevent the Extrovert from swaying opinions with rumors.

Becoming Defensive
Behavior:
If their reputation or status with their work group is threatened, Extroverts can become openly aggressive or defensive. Either way, the reaction will be emotional.

Response:
When you must relay negative information that will affect an Extrovert's standing within a group, try to offer one or two ways for the Extrovert to save face. Sharing the blame with yourself or some external situation may be sufficient to keep an Extrovert under control, as in this example:

■ Ted's sales figures are down this month, but this time of year is often slow for his territory.

5

61

Hiding Their True Feelings
Behavior:

When you're dealing with Extroverts, appearance isn't necessarily reality. They hide behind their good nature and may seem agreeable and compliant while undermining an action or policy. Spreading rumors and gossiping are common methods Extroverts use to gain control. Sabotage is a possibility.

Response:

Getting Extroverts to discuss issues openly will often lead them to reveal their true feelings. Ask lots of open questions, and let them know you value their opinions. If you don't believe you're getting a complete answer, ask them directly for disagreement or dissenting opinions. Once their position or actions are revealed, Extroverts generally become more cooperative.

> Getting Extroverts to discuss issues openly will often lead them to reveal their true feelings.

Talking Too Much
Behavior:

In conversations or meetings, Extroverts sometimes get so wound up they can't stop talking. They may wander off the topic and get sidetracked. They often overemphasize a point with exaggeration, excessive examples, and supporting stories. Others in the group quickly become irritated.

Response:

Ask Extroverts focusing questions, like "What happened then?" or "What was the final result?" Keep them on track by asking for their point, a summary, or applications of their point. As a last resort, just interrupt them. It may seem rude, but they're used to it.

Having Difficulty Concentrating
Behavior:

Extroverts can apply themselves to a task for about an hour before needing a break. When Extroverts need a change, they can become the kind of drop-in visitors that are hard to get rid of.

Response:
Stand up when Extroverts enter so they feel uncomfortable sitting down. Keep them on their feet, and ask them why they have come by or what they need. Create a reason to have to leave, or as a last resort, just tell them that you don't have time to talk right now and schedule a later time.

Listening Poorly and Making Errors
Behavior:
When someone brings up a new topic, Extroverts can become so concerned about how to respond that they stop listening. They often interrupt to make their point.

Response:
Ask Extroverts to summarize your request or the point you just made. Better yet, ask them how they intend to apply what you just discussed. The embarrassment of not being able to respond will make them better listeners on the next encounter.

Refusing to Comply with Instructions, Rules, or Policies
Behavior:
Extroverts' aversion to restricted freedom leads them to apply their creativity to beating the system. They're really good at it!

Response:
Use direct confrontation and discipline if necessary. Once they know you're on to them, they will go back to trying to please and help you.

Creating Disorganization and Clutter
Behavior:
To an Extrovert, anything with a flat surface is fair game for storage—even the floor. They think that if they can't see it, it's gone. Putting things in drawers scares them, so piles and stacks build up quickly. Amazingly, they can function this way fairly effectively, but the appearance soon reaches critical mass.

5

Extroverts often apply their creativity to beating the system.

Response:
You can create more open surfaces by providing worktables, credenzas, etc., but eventually Extroverts have to start putting things away. Set expectations for use of files and storage boxes. Teach them to keep only those items that can be used for planning or control. Counseling from an organization consultant may help.

Arriving Late
Behavior:
Extroverts get so wrapped up with other people that they lose track of time, especially if they're helping someone. Frequent late arrivals at meetings and appointments harm credibility and customer relations.

> Extroverts get so wrapped up with other people that they lose track of time.

Response:
Set up a reward system for timeliness. The reward doesn't matter as much as the fact that you expect promptness and will be upset if they're late. Don't hesitate to show displeasure one-on-one, and bring group pressure to bear if necessary. On one team, each member threw a quarter in a kitty if their Extrovert arrived on time. If the Extrovert was late, the Extrovert had to throw in a dollar. Kitty money was used for a party.

Extroverts' creativity, their ability to work with others, and their desire to please can make them pleasant employees to work with and supervise. Take advantage of their abilities by assigning work that builds on those strengths and provides the variety they crave.

Take a Moment

Ethyl is the unofficial office social director. She is constantly flitting from desk to desk "just to say hi" or "just dropping by." You suspect that most of the many rumors in the workplace originate or are passed on through Ethyl. She is often late for work and takes long breaks. The work of others is affected, and some have complained. Amazingly, the work she generates is above average in quality and quantity. You wonder what she could accomplish with focused effort!

Ethyl is great with customers, and everyone seems to like her. The other day, she appeared at your door with three other employees and said that she represented the feelings of many other workers in regard to a problem with poor equipment in the break room.

Reviewing the response tips above, how would you work with Ethyl?

_____

_____

_____

_____

_____

5

Here's one way to handle the situation in the previous exercise. One of the keys to working with Extroverts is that they want to please and be liked by others. Meet with Ethyl alone and state that you and her coworkers are angry and disappointed with her interruptions and gossip. Write clear expectations for her future behavior. Coach at every opportunity, and you should see a change in Ethyl's behavior with having to take disciplinary action.

As for the equipment request, have Ethyl justify the request with facts and figures and give you a written recommendation. Stay objective, explain your decision to everyone, and compliment your employees on their efforts to improve the workplace.

Chapter Summary

Extroverts can provide the spice of life for your organization.

Extroverts can provide the spice of life for your organization. They are filled with ideas and creativity and enjoy working with and helping others. They have good communication skills and remain optimistic even in difficult situations.

Because of their outgoing nature, Extroverts sometimes find it hard to remain focused on one task for too long or to listen carefully when receiving directions. They may also have difficulty following rules and keeping their workplace free of clutter.

You can help your Extrovert employees succeed by providing them with a variety of tasks that engage their creativity and allow them to work with people rather than figures. Whenever possible, recognize and compliment their efforts and be attentive when they offer opinions and advice. Check to see that Extroverts are listening by asking them to paraphrase what you just said, and don't be afraid to confront them about following rules and procedures.

Self-Check: Chapter Five Review

Answers to these questions appear on page 110.

1. Which of the following is not an Extrovert trait?
   a. Loves to meet people.
   b. Enjoys repetitive tasks.
   c. Is creative and innovative.
   d. Excels in team situations.

2. True or False?
   Because they are so outgoing, Extroverts need little
   appreciation or affirmation from others.

3. True or False?
   Extroverts can't deal with competitive situations because they
   can't stand to lose.

4. If their status within their work group is threatened,
   Extroverts can become defensive. How can you relay
   negative information to an Extrovert in front of a group
   without generating this response?

   _____

   _____

   _____

5. True or False?
   In conversations or meetings, Extroverts sometimes get so
   wound up they can't stop talking.

5

Chapter *Six*

Supervising the Patient Personality

Chapter Objectives

▶ Identify and understand the Patient type.

▶ Recognize difficult Patient behavior.

▶ Prevent difficult Patient behavior, and deal with it effectively when it does occur.

"**B**ut I don't want to change offices," Danielle announced when she heard that her department would move to a new facility. "They've already switched my cubicle twice this year, and now we'll be sent to a completely different building. This will change everything—the way I drive to work, the place I park. And I hate having movers handling my things. At least they could have given us some advance warning!"

Identifying Patient Traits

Fifty percent of the general population will have their highest score on the Patient type.

Watch carefully, because 50 percent of the general population will have their highest score on the Patient type. This is very important for identifying personality traits in others, because half of everyone you meet is in this category. One sensible rule would be to treat everyone you meet like a Patient person until proven otherwise. Since this is also the trait that blends with others the most often, there's about a 70 percent chance that you'll be relating to a person's primary or secondary trait with this approach.

Patients are very easygoing and likable people. Their pace is steady, and they like a stable, secure, and predictable environment. Patients are very loyal and would be content to work for the same company their whole life and build up a hefty retirement program. Moving and job changes are very disruptive to them.

When working with others, they want to see harmony and cooperation because they hate conflict. Patients are timely, dependable, and have a high need for order. Some more of their normal behaviors follow:

◆ On the People vs. Tasks scale, Patients are well balanced, with a little more emphasis on people.

◆ Patients are excellent listeners. They prefer that others state their opinions first so that when it's their turn, they can make their point without offending.

◆ Patients have a calming, soft demeanor that keeps emotions low-key. They are very good at counseling, mediation, and conflict resolution.

◆ Patients have a keen sense of fairness for themselves and others.

◆ Patients demonstrate an ability to persevere and have great patience during tasks, thus their type name.

◆ Patients value loyalty, whether to a family or the workplace. They stick with something unless there is compelling reason to drop it.

◆ Patients prefer to work on one task at a time, starting and finishing without interruption and performing at a high quality level.

◆ Patients take great pride in applying specialized skills to an established process or workflow.

◆ Patients are especially good at setting priorities and make wise choices when given time for proper consideration.

6

Patients value loyalty, whether to a family or the workplace.

♦ Patients are highly intuitive to people and sensitive to environmental factors, such as heat, light, noise, odors, tastes, color, and texture.

Patients are possessive of projects and possessions.

♦ Patients are possessive of projects and possessions. Items at work are referred to as "theirs," and they put their names on tools and desk accessories.

Frequent Patient career choices include nursing and other health occupations, counseling, social work, construction, repair and maintenance, administrative support, assembly line work, engineering, accounting, insurance, stockbrokerage, and law.

Recent Patient presidents include John Kennedy most of the time, Gerald Ford, and George Bush. The Patient type is a secondary trait of Bill Clinton.

Patient public figures include many actors and actresses, such as Glenn Close and Sean Connery, Steve Forbes, Billy Graham, Walter Cronkite, Al Gore, Joe Montana, Arnold Palmer, and Bob Dole.

Take a Moment

List the names of people you know at work and in your personal life who display Patient traits:

_____

_____

_____

_____

Preventing Patients from Becoming Difficult

It takes a great deal of poor treatment to make a Patient person difficult. We have seen that at their core, they desire harmony and peacefulness. The following tips can be used to maintain their normally lovable nature:

What Patients Like

◆ Strive for fair treatment. Explain the pros and cons of your choices or actions.

◆ Be considerate, thoughtful, and mannerly. Patients want you to respect them as people.

◆ Provide a steady flow of information about what's going on in the workplace. Answer all the basic questions surrounding an issue.

Prepare Patients for change well in advance of the event.

◆ Prepare Patients for change well in advance of the event. They need time to process the alternatives.

◆ Provide assurance and security with facts, logic, and common sense.

6

◆ Make Patients a part of group activities and show that you trust them with responsibility.

◆ Give them their space and a fairly low-pressure work environment.

What Patients Dislike

◆ Help Patients avoid stress and time pressures, especially when decisions are needed. They need to think things through.

◆ Try to avoid arguments and strife, especially over unimportant issues.

◆ Avoid sudden, disruptive change with no preparation. Patients don't like negative surprises!

◆ Don't hold Patients to expectations without explanations. Make your instructions complete.

Patients hate unfair treatment in any form for themselves and others!

◆ Be sure to treat all employees fairly. Patients hate unfair treatment in any form for themselves and others! That includes judgmental attitudes and manipulative behavior.

◆ Don't threaten Patients' routines. Relocations and changes in job duties are particularly disruptive.

◆ Don't borrow or handle Patients' possessions. Loss, breakage, and messy returned items are very upsetting to them.

Take a Moment

Choose a Patient person in the workplace with whom you would like to improve your relationship. (Write that person's initials here: _____)

From the information just discussed, pick two actions that you will take in order to adapt to his or her behavior and write them below:

1._____

2. _____

Now select two actions that you will avoid doing in order to adapt to his or her behavior and write them below:

1. _____

2. _____

Implement your written plan of action on your next encounter and develop plans of action for other Patient people in your workplace.

Recognizing Typical Patient Difficult Behaviors

You won't see difficult behavior from Patient people very often. However, when they do become difficult, all of their wonderful traits become focused on restoration at best and getting even at worst. Their general difficult behavior is usually cause-based pursuit with dogged determination. They prefer words to weapons and use them with well-planned precision. Here's what to watch for and what to do about it:

Difficult Behaviors and Recommended Responses

Resisting Change
Behavior:
Anything that threatens their situations or relationships is the enemy. "If it ain't broke, don't fix it" is their motto.

Response:
Prepare them for change with all the information you have. If you don't know something, tell them you don't know. If Patients have enough information and time to absorb and incubate, they can become the biggest supporters of your change.

Avoiding Risk
Behavior:
Patients' need for security, stability, and predictability makes risk taking and decision making very difficult. They become overly cautious and defensive. They find even the thought of losing possessions or position frightening.

Response:
Provide all the facts and figures you can and give them time to absorb and work through the options. Look for a more conservative approach as an escape route for them.

Becoming Overloaded with Information
Behavior:
Too much information, chaos, or stress can shut the Patient person down. The Patient response to a six-page restaurant menu will be a compromised order or a long delay for the server.

6

Too much information, chaos, or stress can shut the Patient person down.

Response:
When possible, keep options to two or three choices. Ask some qualifying questions, such as "How important is color compared to price?" Watch the levels of heat, light, noise, ventilation, and traffic in the work environment.

Hoarding Information or Possessions
Behavior:
Trying to maintain possession of desk staplers or vice-grip pliers wouldn't qualify as difficult behavior. However, protecting an "information is power" position by giving certain people only certain bits of information and withholding it from others can be considerably disruptive.

Response:
Insecurity and a desire to be needed are at the core of this behavior. Verbal reassurance of the Patient person's value to the organization is a good first step. Show appreciation when information and control of resources is shared properly. If a Patient person still refuses to share information, directly confront the person regarding the motives for this behavior. See Chapter Eight for details on positive confrontation.

> Patient people do not innovate or jump into things quickly.

Adopting Innovations Slowly
Behavior:
Patient people do not innovate or jump into things quickly. They watch and study the game before attempting to play. As a result, they often start at a skill disadvantage and can become dependent on others who jumped in and learned the hard way. Any criticism only adds to feelings of inadequacy, and self-image plummets. Effects in the workplace may appear as withdrawal, apathy, resistance to change, lack of confidence, and nonparticipation in activities.

Response:
Provide opportunities for small successes, provide training that allows practical application and promotes self-sufficiency, and affirm desired behavior at every opportunity. Provide safety nets for attempts by using mistakes as teaching opportunities, and generate team and coworker support for their capabilities. At a serious enough level, professional counseling may be necessary.

Stating Opinions Indirectly
Behavior:
Patient people are very concerned about upsetting or offending others. As a result, they like to get input and opinions from others before responding. They have an amazing capability to listen, and they even absorb the speaker's phrases and vocabulary. When they state their own opinions, they often do so using the other person's verbiage. They can be so indirect that you may not realize that they didn't agree with you. How can this great skill be difficult behavior? You may not understand how they really feel or what their decision really is.

Response:
First of all, try to get them to go first so that they have to state their own opinion. Watch for them trying to draw you out to take the lead again. If they won't voice their opinions, state yours and then ask them to respond while you listen carefully. Gently pin them down by asking for more information on some of their points. If necessary, confront them by asking them if that is how they really feel, and ask them for alternative positions.

Allowing Delayed Reactions to Build Stress and
Bitterness
Behavior:
When Patient people become upset, they choose to control themselves and delay their response. As the upsetting situation continues, Patient people's senses heighten, especially listening.

They begin preparing their response that night as they lay awake thinking through every detail of what happened. By the end of the second sleepless night, they have memorized their response as well as comebacks for every reaction or defense. The confrontation consists of a calm, cold verbal dissection of the victim. Without raising their voices, Patients are able to verbally cut off all avenues of escape, and the accused are condemned by their own statements, which Patients can recall verbatim.

6

> **When Patient people become upset, they choose to control themselves and delay their response.**

Response:
Maybe the offending parties deserve what they get, but it would be better for both sides if offenders could address the hurt and discuss the resolution when the original situation occurs. When Patient people engage in the scenario described above, try asking them not to delay their response the next time something happens.

Taking Up a Cause or an Offense
Behavior:
Patient people will endure a lot, even some unfair treatment. However, when they realize that they have been treated unfairly or been taken advantage of, and there is no way to resolve it, look out! These kind, warm, sensitive harmony-seeking people will become cause-driven activists fighting against whatever or whoever caused the problem. This is why boycotts are organized. This is why people on strike write "Unfair" at the top of their placards. This is why protesters chain themselves to the gates of nuclear plants and attack fishing fleets in inflatable dinghies.

> Patient people can become cause-driven activists if treated unfairly.

Response:
Prevention is the key! It may sound trite to say treat your staff fairly and don't take advantage of them, but that's the solution. If prevention fails, swiftly negotiate to resolve the issue. The longer the dispute remains, the more determined Patients become.

The Patient personality type brings stability to your organization. Treat Patient people fairly and help them adjust to change, and they will reward you with loyalty and perseverance.

Take a Moment

Patricia is the foundation of your sales team. Her customers are more attached to her than to the products she represents, and you've had nightmares about her going elsewhere. Last week in a sales meeting, the head of Information Services announced some changes that will require salespeople to switch the software that controls their customer database.

Patricia's eyes rolled back in her head during that announcement, and she's been fighting the conversion at every turn. Yesterday she even went directly to the head of I.S. and verbally pinned him against the wall for coming up with this whole idea. You've already gotten a call from him.

The rebellion is spreading, and you fear that this has blown so out of proportion that Patricia may be considering resignation. Reviewing the tips above, what would you do now, and what should have been done to prevent this level of disruption?

_____

_____

_____

_____

6

Here's one approach to the situation in the above exercise: The major causes of Patricia's behaviors are *resisting change, avoiding the risk* of dealing with new software, *overload,* and *taking up a cause.* Patricia needs information about the pros and cons of the new software and time to formulate questions and give feedback. Had this been done earlier, it would have prevented her reactions. Providing it now will restore a sense of fairness and remove the need for a cause. Apologizing to Patricia for the oversight would help, and you should discuss her employment needs to improve the chances of retention.

Chapter Summary

Patient people bring loyalty and stability to your workplace. This personality type shows great patience when working on tasks. They prefer to focus on one task at a time, starting and finishing without interruption and performing at a high-quality level. They are good at setting priorities and have a calming, low-key demeanor that makes them natural counselors and mediators.

Patient people can have difficulty dealing with change and dislike taking risks. They are especially concerned that all people, including themselves, be treated fairly, and will take action against a perceived injustice.

To help Patients succeed in your organization, provide plenty of information whenever a change is about to take place, and allow them to take a conservative approach to innovation. Strive to treat all employees fairly and to quickly resolve any conflicts that do arise.

Self-Check: Chapter Six Review

Answers to the following questions appear on page 110.

1. Which of the following is not a Patient trait?
   a. Has difficulty listening.
   b. Appears calm and low-key.
   c. Prefers to work on one task at a time.
   d. Is possessive of objects and possessions.

2. True or False?
   Patient people are able to deal with large amounts of
   information and stress without becoming overloaded.

3. Patient people are generally uncomfortable with change.
   What can a supervisor do to help them through?

   _____

   _____

   _____

4. True or False?
   Patient people feel comfortable forcefully stating their
   opinions.

6

5. Patient people can become difficult if they perceive that they
   or others are being treated unfairly. How can a supervisor
   handle this situation?

   _____

   _____

Chapter *Seven*

Supervising the Conformist Personality

Chapter Objectives

▶ Identify and understand the Conformist type.

▶ Recognize difficult Conformist behavior.

▶ Prevent difficult Conformist behavior, and deal with it effectively when it does occur.

"**D**ale, we need your part of the proposal right away," Nancy said as she hurried into Dale's office. "It was due over an hour ago, and the boss isn't happy."

"I'll be ready in a minute," Dale answered without looking up from his calculator. "I just want to go over these figures one more time. I think we can be more accurate in our projections."

"But Dale, the proposal has to go out *now*," Nancy responded in exasperation. "The most accurate projections in the world won't do us any good if the client chooses another firm because we can't meet deadlines."

Identifying Conformist Traits

Math problems fascinate Conformists.

If you're a Conformist personality type, you already know that they are the other 15 percent of the general population. Adding percentages from chapter to chapter is the kind of task that fascinates Conformists, as do most math problems. As soon as Conformist readers got the Patient percentage, they probably added the percentages from the first three personality types and quickly subtracted from 100 just to figure a total before turning to this chapter. For you Dominant and Extrovert readers that aren't sure what this is all about, don't worry—you wouldn't care anyway, even if the total were 5 to 10 percent off.

If someone asked for the best word to describe the Conformist type, "quality" would be a good choice. Give them a process to follow and a standard of achievement, and your supervisory worries are over. They will perform 20 to 30 percent above your expectations just to prevent criticism. They are the most introverted of the four traits, but when they do speak, it's usually profound. Their cautions are usually well founded in fact and experience and should be heeded. Some of their other normal behaviors follow:

◆ On the task vs. people scale, Conformists are balanced, with some preference for tasks.

◆ Conformists focus on detail at a level of precision far beyond the Patient person's focus. These are the people who win trivia contests, and they have facts five levels deep.

◆ The Conformist ability to analyze something or someone is uncanny. They seem to have a very accurate intuition of what makes people and things work.

The Conformist ability to analyze something or someone is uncanny.

◆ The Conformist orientation to processes and systems is so strong that results become a by-product. W. Edwards Deming, the father of continuous process improvement, was a Conformist.

◆ Conformists have the courage to caution you or try to slow you down if they feel you are heading in the wrong direction or not being careful.

7

◆ Conformists may not say much at all, and when they do, they are diplomatic and tactful.

◆ Conformists are respectful of authority. They prefer a controlled environment free of stress and chaos. They enjoy following directions and standards.

◆ Conformists tend to withdraw during stress and conflict.

◆ Conformists show a tremendous concern for accuracy and doing things the right way.

Frequent Conformist career choices include health-care technologists or technicians, auditors, specialist engineers, airline pilots, cost accountants, government compliance positions, college professors, machinists, computer programmers, positions requiring mathematics and statistics, researchers and financial specialists, such as actuaries.

Recent Conformist presidents include Jimmy Carter and Dwight Eisenhower.

Conformist public figures include Henry Kissinger, Alan Greenspan, William Buckley, most classical music artists and conductors (Bernstein, Perlman), most Supreme Court justices, and athletes in technical sports, like gymnastics, golf, and sailing.

Take a Moment

List the names of people you know at work and in your personal life who display Conformist traits:

_____

_____

_____

_____

Preventing Conformists from Becoming Difficult

Conformists' desire to be tactful and diplomatic while maintaining emotional control keeps them from being difficult most of the time. However, they have some tactics that can be difficult when applied in a different way.

What Conformists Like

◆ Provide Conformists with factual information and knowledge. Explain all topics thoroughly and provide written materials with references. They want to know exactly what's expected of them.

◆ Emphasize quality at all stages of effort. Not all Conformists are perfectionists, but they will not associate with slack or incomplete efforts.

◆ Ask for and respect their opinions. Often, if they're not asked, they won't tell. Their concerns will be fact-based, and you need to know what they are. Ask your questions in a one-on-one informal environment, and don't interrupt their reply.

When speaking to Conformists, maintain a calm and respectful demeanor.

◆ When speaking to Conformists, maintain a calm and respectful demeanor. Keep your own emotions under control.

◆ Allow Conformists ample physical space and restrict physical contact. Conformists are not touchy-feely.

◆ Provide Conformists with a clean and comfortable working environment with clear policies and procedures.

7

◆ Give Conformists sincere and factual appreciation for their efforts and results. One mild commendation will motivate a Conformist for a month.

What Conformists Dislike

◆ Avoid making generalities or giving vague instructions.

◆ Avoid emotional outbursts and mean-spirited treatment. Conformists strive for self-control, and they expect you to as well.

◆ Do not personally attack Conformists, blame them, or criticize their work. If you attack Conformists, they will remember every detail of what you did and said for the next five years (and what you were wearing when it happened).

♦ Don't subject Conformists to frequent transfers. Avoid interrupting them when they are working or speaking. Finishing projects, statements, and thoughts is important to Conformists, and they become frustrated when interrupted.

♦ Don't ask Conformists to take shortcuts or violate policies or procedures. You'll lose their respect.

Don't subject Conformists to rapid change or rush their work.

♦ Don't subject Conformists to rapid change or rush their work. Speed and quality are contradictory for them. They will take much longer to complete paperwork than others, but they won't have to do it over. Be patient.

♦ Don't force Conformists into direct competition with others. They enjoy a challenge, but they like to work against the clock, their own previous performance, or impersonal situations, like wind and water conditions, courses, and equipment.

Take a Moment

Choose a Conformist person in the workplace with whom you would like to improve your relationship. (Write that person's initials here:_____)

From the information just discussed, pick two actions that you will take in order to adapt to his or her behavior and write them below:

1. _____

2. _____

Now select two actions that you will avoid doing in order to adapt to his or her behavior and write them below:

1. _____

2. _____

Implement your written plan of action on your next encounter and develop plans of action for other Conformist people in your workplace.

Recognizing Typical Conformist Difficult Behaviors

When Conformists become difficult, you won't see much difference in their behavior, but you'll feel the effects. In general, they use their tremendous grasp of detail and facts as a restraining force. You'll feel the drag! For example, a Conformist with a copy of *Robert's Rules of Order* can completely paralyze a meeting. Other tactics they might use and how you should respond follows:

Difficult Behaviors and Recommended Responses

Taking a Negative Approach to Change
Behavior:
This is referred to as "the voice crying in the wilderness" syndrome. While everyone else is heading out for action, you'll hear, "Excuse me, but that won't work," or "I think you need more research first." This can be frustrating, and you may be tempted simply to ignore their warnings.

Response:
Stop and ask for an explanation. Conformists won't speak up if they can't defend their position, and they're trying to get your attention long enough to explain. They have a valid point, so listen. If you choose to ignore them, they'll let you go and run right off a cliff with some remark like, "I tried to warn them," which they did.

> Conformists won't speak up if they can't defend their position.

Using Facts to Restrain
Behavior:
If you try to take Conformists where they don't want to go, they will begin to bury you with facts and data as to why you shouldn't do that.

Response:
Stay objective and listen. Conformists don't usually take this approach unless they're sure they're right, so you might learn something and avoid some trouble. If you still need to go against their wishes, thank them for their input, give them credit for their extensive knowledge, and tell them why you must do things differently. Good luck!

Focusing on Process, Not Results

7

Behavior:

Conformists sometimes place too much emphasis on procedures. To them, how something is done is much more important than the results. Completing the task without following the proper procedure isn't satisfying because it wasn't done properly. This can drive a task-oriented Dominant supervisor up a wall.

> Conformists sometimes place too much emphasis on procedures.

Response:

Keep reinforcing completion and results. Assure Conformists that perfection isn't necessary in order to achieve completion. Show appreciation and encouragement when you get the desired behavior.

Complaining
Behavior:

If Conformists are required to do something they don't like or don't agree with, you'll hear about it at every event that confirms their position. They don't yell or scream, but they do provide nerve-grating, whining reminders that they were right, and it can drive a supervisor crazy.

Response:

You can tell Conformists to stop complaining, but you run the risk of losing their input altogether. Instead, try asking how they would achieve the desired results. Because Conformists are often focused on process, they may not have thought about results, so having to generate new solutions can force them to look at the situation from the supervisor's position and become a little more positive and results-oriented.

Maintaining a Slow Pace
Behavior:

Conformists' drive to get it right the first time overrides time requirements. They will often study a situation longer than it takes others to complete their response. They hate being rushed and asked to compromise quality.

Response:
Calmly and factually explain the deadline. Explain that getting the project done exactly right doesn't matter if it is done late and is rejected by the customer. Set up rewards for timely completion if appropriate.

Focusing on Minutia
Behavior:
When Conformists are working on something they really like, they can spend a lot of time going off on tangents that won't really affect the project outcome. Sometimes, their efforts can remind others of the feeling one gets after completing a crossword puzzle. It was a great effort requiring a lot of knowledge, but what are you going to do with it?

Response:
Continually coach Conformists and communicate expectations in terms of results and outcomes. They will strive to exceed expectations if they know and understand them.

> Conformists
> will strive
> to exceed
> expectations
> if they know
> and understand
> them.

Demanding Extra Instructions and Attention
Behavior:
Conformists don't want to begin a project until they thoroughly understand it. They want all basic questions answered, including the dreaded "Why?" questions. They will also ask for confirmation throughout the project. "Is this what you want?" or "Is this right?" or "What do I do next?" are common questions.

Response:
Provide Conformists with all the necessary information the first time you assign a task, and inform them that they are to apply this information to future projects without further explanation. Commend them when they apply what they've learned without asking you to reward the correct behavior.

Conformists' emphasis on quality and attention to detail can help your organization produce superior products and services. Make the most of your Conformist employees by giving them the time and space they need to complete their projects with as few interruptions as possible. At the same time, help them keep the big picture in mind so that they don't get so bogged down in details that they forget to consider results.

7

Take a Moment

Carl is your chief plant technician. You are planning a new facility with some progressive, fast-tracking architects. Carl's input has been invaluable, but he has had trouble getting the architects to accept his ideas or pay attention to his suggestions.

Last week, they submitted their specifications for the equipment and the assembly line process. Carl was visibly shaken at the presentation but didn't say anything. This morning, Carl laid on your desk a six-inch high stack of brochures and a 35-page report on alternative equipment and processes that he knows are superior. In his report, he called the architect's suggestions unacceptable, and he has asked you to present the information to the architects. How do you handle the situation?

_____

_____

_____

_____

_____

How would you deal with the previous scenario? You have just been bombarded with a pile of facts designed to *get attention* and *restrain further action*. Conformists rarely take a stand like this unless they know they're right. If Carl is right, the next question is "so what?" Right isn't always feasible, and quality isn't always affordable. Supply Carl's information to the architects and set up a meeting with them so both sides can present their views. Keep asking, "Is the higher quality worth the cost?" It's not uncommon to have Conformists on your staff who know more than outside experts. Listen to them.

Chapter Summary

Conformists have a natural love of accuracy, quality, and precision that makes them naturals at detailed work. They have a strong orientation toward processes and systems and great skill at in-depth analysis.

Conformists are naturals at detailed work.

Because of their love of detail, Conformists can become so focused on process that they forget to consider results. They sometimes head off on tangents that, while interesting, add little value to their current project. They dislike being interrupted and can have difficulty adapting to change.

To work effectively with Conformist employees, provide them with clear information and instructions and fully explain your expectations. Emphasize results, and listen to their opinions when they disagree with a decision. Provide them with a clean, comfortable work environment, and let them know that you value their efforts.

7

Self-Check: Chapter Seven Review

Answers to the following questions appear on pages 110 and 111.

1. Which of the following is not a Conformist trait?
   a. Diplomatic and tactful.
   b. Focused on detail.
   c. Concerned with accuracy.
   d. Unable to work with rules and authority.

2. True or False?
   Conformists can become chronic complainers if forced to do something they don't want to do.

3. True or False?
   Conformists strive for self-control but don't mind emotional outbursts in others.

4. Conformists often take a negative approach to change and feel the need to tell their supervisors why specific proposals won't work. How should supervisors handle such situations?

   _____

   _____

   _____

5. True or False?
   Conformists enjoy competing against their coworkers to see who can achieve the best results.

Notes

Chapter *Eight*

Dealing with Difficult Behaviors Based in Experience

Chapter Objectives

▶ Identify difficult behaviors that result from a person's life experiences.

▶ Coach employees to improve experience-related difficult behaviors.

▶ Use your organization's discipline and termination procedures when employees refuse to change difficult behaviors.

❝I don't know why we bother to show up here every day, anyway." Ralph said as he slid in place behind his machine. "We're just rats in a cage to management. They work us till we drop, then pay us peanuts. Now they want us to learn all new procedures. I tell you, one of these days, I'm going to take a permanent sick leave."

"I wish he would and do us all a favor," Hector whispered to Sandy. "The only bad thing about working here is his constant whining."

In previous chapters, we saw that all behavior, difficult or otherwise, is based in a combination of hereditary factors and life experiences. Together, heredity and experience form the relational system that we refer to as an individual's personality.

Together, heredity and experience form the relational system that we refer to as an individual's personality.

As we have seen, many difficult behaviors can be traced to personality. We can effectively respond to these difficult behaviors by adjusting to an individual's personality type. However, there are a number of difficult behaviors that we haven't accounted for yet.

Some life experiences have such an impact that they create a set of behaviors that transcend the personality categories. The personality may affect how the experiences are perceived, but the human response across all categories is about the same.

> **Some life experiences have such an impact that they create a set of behaviors that transcend the personality categories.**

For example, consider a young child who experiences the death of a parent. The child's personality may cause some variations in how that individual responds, but any child will go through the grieving process. In the years to come, the child will adapt to the loss and compensate in a number of common ways. Most would develop an advanced level of independence simply because they had to do more themselves, especially if there are younger siblings. Even though independent action may be a natural tendency for Dominants or Conformists, we may now see it in the behaviors of Extroverts and Patients because of the experience.

The event could also cause some common difficult behaviors. We might see a child who had lost a parent develop bitterness or jealousy against a child raised with both parents, especially if the child with both parents excelled academically, won a contest, or made a sports team. In later life, these same feelings may appear as a subconscious prejudice against coworkers who come from traditional homes. Such coworkers could receive hostile or unfair treatment from the difficult person and never understand its source.

8

Identifying Experience-Based Difficult Behavior

We can identify a number of different types of experience-based difficult behaviors, including:

- ◆ Dishonesty

- ◆ Treating others unfairly

- ◆ Self-centeredness

- ◆ Jealousy

- ◆ Apathy and uncooperativeness

- ◆ Disrespect

- ◆ Negativity or bitterness

After we describe some of the specific behaviors associated with each type, we will consider some techniques for effectively dealing with them.

Dishonesty

Dishonesty in the workplace stems from an absence of values and the ability to justify immoral behavior.

Dishonesty in the workplace stems from an absence of values and the ability to justify immoral behavior. The clear line between right and wrong that previous generations were raised with has eroded into a wide gray river of "it all depends" situational ethics. This type of thinking can lead to such difficult behaviors as lying, theft, fraud, embezzlement, bribes, violation of contracts or noncompetition agreements, and cheating suppliers or customers.

Treating Others Unfairly

Most people want to succeed and enjoy the benefits of that success. There's nothing wrong with advancing our own careers as long as we also treat others fairly and build them up along the way. But the desire to succeed creates difficult behavior when people take advantage of others and attempt to profit at their expense. The results of such behavior can be loss of respect, lack of trust, fear, and anxiety.

Self-Centeredness

Just as each of us wants to succeed, we also want to preserve our own well-being. When we confront an issue, it's normal to ask ourselves:

- How will this affect my situation?

- How will this affect my relationships?

There is nothing wrong with asking these questions, but when people think only of their own self-interests, their extreme self-focus creates difficult behavior. Self-centered people are unable to make sacrifices, take risks, or work effectively on teams. They constantly demand better work assignments, promotions, or raises, which can be frustrating for a supervisor.

> Self-centered people are unable to make sacrifices, take risks, or work effectively on teams.

Jealousy

Jealousy is closely related to self-centeredness. It occurs when one person believes that he or she should be enjoying another person's success. If the jealous person can't get what the other person has, he or she may try to ruin that person's achievements. This can lead to such difficult behaviors as spreading rumors and gossip or undermining another's work. Jealousy is often the motive when an employee tries to get a supervisor in trouble or fired.

Apathy and Uncooperativeness

Some people project an attitude that says, "I don't care," or "You can't do anything to me." Perhaps these people truly dislike their work or view it as insignificant, or perhaps they have experienced so much personal failure that they have developed a negative self-image. Whatever its source, this type of difficult behavior shows a lack of loyalty and commitment to the workplace and can destroy the morale of other employees.

8

Disrespectfulness

Disrespectfulness can include such difficult behaviors as abusing coworkers' rights and company property. It can also involve a refusal to respect rules and authority. This type of behavior can lead to hostility between coworkers, the neglect or damage of equipment, injury, and even sabotage.

Negativity or Bitterness

A chronic negative attitude complete with complaining and whining becomes as grating as fingernails on a blackboard. This type of behavior often shows up when change is needed. If nothing shakes a person out of this approach, it degenerates into bitterness and even hatred.

Take a Moment

Think of a situation in which you saw an employee engage in one of the types of difficult behaviors just listed. What are some of the specific behaviors you observed? List them below.

_____   _____

_____   _____

_____   _____

Responding to Experience-Based Difficult Behavior

When supervisors experience the types of difficult behaviors just described, how should they respond? In the last four chapters, we saw that by changing our own behaviors and/or the work environment, we could work more effectively with people whose difficult behavior was based in personality. The options for dealing with experience-based difficult behaviors are the same, but the tools and responses are not.

As supervisors who are responsible for productivity, we must recognize improper behavior rooted in bad experiences and work within the law and organizational policy to respond. We should begin with a positive approach in order to help the employee change the negative behavior, but we may have to resort to stronger tactics if a positive approach isn't successful.

The process for responding to experience-based difficult behavior includes these steps:

Step 1: *Coach* the employee and motivate him or her to change the difficult behavior.

Step 2: If the employee refuses to change his or her behavior, begin the *disciplinary process.* Consult with your organization's Human Resources Department to learn the steps your organization follows.

Step 3: If the employee still refuses to change, or if the difficult behavior involves a serious issue, such as stealing, take the final step of *termination.* The major problem most supervisors have in dealing with experience-based difficult behavior is that they complete Steps 1 and 2 but cannot bring themselves to take Step 3, so they just tolerate the behavior. Termination is never pleasant, but consider this: Tolerating truly difficult behavior destroys the morale of other employees and lowers their performance and productivity.

Now we'll consider each of the steps in detail, beginning with Step 1.

Step 1: Playing the Role of Coach

How do you tell another person that you're having trouble with his or her behavior? One approach is to adopt the role of a coach. Behaving like a good athletic coach is part of an overall management style that moves the supervisor away from just directing people. Coaching allows for increased employee input and increased delegation of authority to solve problems and make decisions.

> Coaching allows for increased employee input and increased delegation of authority to solve problems and make decisions.

8

Many books and other instructional materials are available on coaching, so we will not try to give a full description of the process here. Instead, we will provide a brief overview of some coaching techniques, then consider how coaches can use those techniques when helping an employee correct difficult behavior.

Common Coaching Techniques

◆ **Be with the team.**
A good coaching supervisor should be visible. Coaches practice on the field or court, not in the locker room. If your staff doesn't see you because you spend all your time in your office, they conclude that you don't care about their performance (even if you do).

◆ **Communicate constantly.**
Coaches don't get paid to be quiet, and neither do supervisors. If you frequently visit with individual staff members, you will be able to address problems as they occur—before they get blown out of proportion.

◆ **Provide both positive and corrective feedback.**
When staff members perform above expectations, let them know—a simple verbal statement is usually sufficient. This positive feedback provides a balance for the corrective feedback you need to give when problems arise.

> **When providing corrective feedback, don't criticize the employee or attack his or her character.**

When providing corrective feedback, don't criticize the employee or attack his or her character. Instead, work with the employee to develop a plan for correcting the problem and preventing it in the future. Follow up to be sure the employee is putting the plan into action. Remember, good coaches don't just yell at their team—they explain how to improve skills and run the plays better.

Confronting the Difficult Behavior

So how does a supervisor coach an employee to change difficult behavior? Follow the steps below:

1. Approach the employee and ask if this is a good time to talk. If the employee is involved in something and can't break away, arrange to talk later. If the employee is available, move to a quiet, neutral setting (not your own office) where you can talk without being overheard.

2. Once you and the employee are situated, describe the difficult behavior that you have observed or had reported. Focus on the observable behavior—not the employee's attitude or character—and be as specific as possible in your descriptions, as in this example:

> **Focus on the observable behavior—not the employee's attitude or character.**

■ Yesterday evening, Teresa asked you to help her clean off the grill, and you refused. You also refused to help Emilio when he asked you to help him total receipts on Tuesday night, and you've been late to work twice this week.

3. Explain the effects the difficult behavior is having on customers, fellow employees, and the workplace.

4. Express how you feel about the behavior and any other concerns that it is generating.

5. Describe specifically what you want the employee to do in the future. Don't criticize the employee's attitude or character or dwell on past behaviors. Ask for the employee's feedback, and be sure the employee understands what he or she is supposed to do.

6. Get the employee to agree to the new behavior you have outlined and thank the employee for taking the time to discuss the issue.

7. Document your conversation with the employee so you will be able to trace the employee's progress. Include the date, time, and content of the conversation. Such documentation will be especially useful if you need to resort to discipline or termination later on.

8

8. Follow up with the employee to be sure she or he is practicing the new behavior. Provide further coaching and feedback as needed, and document your follow-up efforts.

9. If the employee doesn't agree to try the new behavior or becomes argumentative, explain the consequences of noncompliance according to your organization's disciplinary policy. Begin discipline and termination procedures as needed.

Let's see how these steps work together in the following example.

Case Study: The Confrontation Process

Steps	Text
1	MANAGER: Hi, Jake, can you break away long enough to talk about something?
	EMPLOYEE: Yeah, sure, what is it?
	MANAGER: Well, lately I've noticed that your error rate has been going up, and as I've watched you, you seem to be distracted, moving slowly, and not responsive to encouragement. Is something wrong?
	EMPLOYEE: No, but it does get boring around here sometimes.
2	MANAGER: Well, I just want you to know that it's causing some of the other staff to resent you for not carrying your weight. The increased error rate could affect the quarterly bonus.
3	MANAGER: I believe it's in your best interest to snap out of this disinterested behavior, get the work done, and salvage the respect of your coworkers.
4	MANAGER: You need to pay closer attention to what you're doing and try to increase your work rate without increasing your error rate. Be a little more personable with the rest of the staff. Is there anything that I can do to help?
5	EMPLOYEE: Well, I could use a break in the routine once in a while, and I guess I should cut down on the night life and get a little more sleep.
	MANAGER: You do that, and I'll make some arrangements to get you cross-training for some variety. I'll check with you later if you have any other needs and to see how you're doing. Thanks for the talk.

Take a Moment

Do you have an employee with experience-based difficult behaviors whom you need to coach? Imagine yourself in the coaching situation and write out your own dialog for dealing with this difficult person:

Step 1

_____

_____

Step 2

_____

_____

Step 3

_____

_____

Step 4

_____

_____

Step 5

_____

_____

Step 6

_____

_____

8

Step 2: Discipline

Sometimes, employees refuse to admit that their difficult behavior is a problem. If an employee refuses to accept your feedback and continues with the difficult behavior, you will need to begin the disciplinary process.

Though every organization has its own disciplinary policy, the process generally consists of a series of steps that can lead to termination. Some typical steps include:

1. Oral warning.

2. Written warning.

3. Suspension.

4. Termination.

Each step of the disciplinary process must be carefully documented.

The disciplinary process provides a formal way for you to warn employees that their behavior is not acceptable. Each step of the disciplinary process must be carefully documented in order to be legally defensible. Consult with your Human Resources Department to learn the specific steps your organization follows and how they should be documented.

Take a Moment

Do you know your organization's disciplinary policy? If not, or if you haven't reviewed it in a while, visit your Human Resources Department and ask for a copy of the policy.

Step 3: Termination

Some behaviors, such as stealing and sabotage, are so serious that you will need to bypass coaching and discipline and go directly to the termination step. In less serious situations, termination comes as a last resort after you have exhausted your coaching and discipline options. Whatever the situation, you should consult with your Human Resources Department to determine your organization's termination policy and procedures.

Conducting the Termination Meeting

The following tips will help you make your termination meeting with the employee as painless as possible:

◆ Don't discipline or terminate an employee in front of other workers. It's embarrassing and may turn the other workers against you. Counsel in private.

◆ Privacy does not mean conducting the termination by yourself—you could run the risk of personal harm if the terminated employee becomes violent. Arrange to have another supervisor or a member of Human Resources with you as a silent witness, and, in extreme cases, arrange to have security staff close by in case of trouble.

◆ Don't succumb to the terminated employee's emotional pleas or arguments. Remember, you gave the employee a chance to correct the behavior. You're not acting out of a personal grudge against the employee; you're simply carrying out the required company policy for that person's actions.

◆ Never terminate an employee on Friday afternoon. A natural inclination for an employee terminated at this time of day is to head to the nearest bar, creating the potential for spouse, child, or pet abuse. Plus, the terminated employee will have an entire weekend to dwell on the situation, perhaps calling former coworkers to complain.

> **Never terminate an employee on Friday afternoon.**

When you must terminate, do so on Monday, Tuesday, Wednesday, or Thursday at 11:45 a.m. This gives the terminated employee a change to gather personal effects over the lunch hour and have the rest of the afternoon to look for a job while the bars are closed.

◆ Accompany terminated employees until they leave company property. Watch them clean out their personal effects so they don't clean you out or say inappropriate things to coworkers. When left unattended, terminated employees can crash hard drives, take customer lists, and sabotage equipment. If they get hurt in the process, your organization will be liable for workers' compensation. Once terminated employees are out of the gate, they are private citizens subject to trespassing laws.

8

◆ Use the understanding gained from this book to establish some selection criteria and hire a great replacement!

At the risk of repeating an earlier point, one of the biggest problems with employment termination is that it isn't done often enough. Nothing destroys staff morale and lowers productivity more than tolerating difficult behavior. Follow your organization's procedures, however restrictive they may be, complete your documentation, and discharge the employee.

Take a Moment

Are you familiar with your organization's termination policy? Don't wait until you have to terminate someone to review it! Visit your Human Resources Department and ask for a copy of the policy.

Dealing with Employee Substance Abuse

Employee substance abuse can create serious consequences for your organization. Besides the obvious problems of low productivity and poor performance, employees who abuse drugs and alcohol engage in a variety of difficult behaviors, such as being overly aggressive or even violent. They may also create safety hazards for themselves and other employees.

Employees who abuse drugs and alcohol engage in a variety of difficult behaviors.

How should a supervisor handle a substance abuse situation? Organizational policies vary. In some situations, you may need to ask the employee to leave the work area or take a drug test if you think he or she is creating a hazard.

As with any mental health issue, you should never attempt to serve as a counselor for an employee with a substance abuse problem. Instead, use the coaching process to describe observable problem behaviors and state that you suspect they may be due to substance abuse. Provide descriptions of specific, observable behaviors, as in this example:

■ David, you came back an hour late from lunch yesterday. You fell asleep at your desk shortly after you got back, and two employees told me they smelled liquor on your breath. Last Friday, several people noticed that after lunch, you were having trouble walking straight, and they also smelled liquor on your breath. I'm beginning to think that you might have a drinking problem.

Follow the coaching process to let the employee know that this type of behavior will not be tolerated. You cannot force an employee to seek counseling, but you can certainly suggest that the employee seek professional help to deal with the problem. If your organization has an employee assistance program that provides counseling, help the employee get in touch with someone who can assist him or her.

Though you may sympathize with an employee who has a substance abuse problem, you cannot allow this type of difficult behavior to continue unchecked. If the employee does not seek help and the behavior continues, you must follow the steps of discipline and termination as you would with any other problem employee. Consult with a member of your Human Resources Department for specific information on how your organization would handle the situation.

You should never attempt to serve as a counselor for an employee with a substance abuse problem.

8

Chapter Summary

A number of difficult behaviors are based in experience rather than heredity. These difficult behaviors can be found in any personality type. Some common types of experience-based difficult behaviors include:

◆ Dishonesty

◆ Treating others unfairly

◆ Self-centeredness

◆ Jealousy

◆ Apathy and uncooperativeness

◆ Disrespect

◆ Negativity or bitterness

Supervisors can help employees change these difficult behaviors by using the coaching process to confront the difficult behavior and develop a solution. If an employee refuses to change the problem behavior, supervisors should follow their organization's disciplinary and termination procedures to deal with the situation. Supervisors can also use the steps of coaching, discipline, and termination to deal with employee substance abuse.

Conclusion

We've considered a variety of difficult behaviors and the factors that cause them. As much as we would like to work in an environment free of difficult behavior, whenever people work together in groups, someone is bound to rub someone else the wrong way. Keep this book handy for future reference. The next time you encounter difficult behavior, diagnose the source, take the recommended actions, and you should have a lot more time to refocus your effort toward productive activity. You should also see more productivity and improved morale in your workforce.

Self-Check: Chapter Eight Review

Answers to the following questions appear on page 111.

1. Dishonesty in the workplace stems from an absence of
   _____ and the ability to justify _____
   behavior.

2. This type of difficult behavior often shows up when change
   is needed.

   _____

3. What are the three steps for dealing with experience-based
   difficult behavior?

   Step 1: _____

   Step 2: _____

   Step 3: _____

4. When confronting an employee about difficult behavior, a
   supervisor should focus on the observable behavior, not the
   employee's _____ or _____.

5. Give two reasons why it is important to document any
   conversation you have with an employee regarding difficult
   behavior.

   _____

   _____

8

Answers to Chapter Reviews

Chapter One (page 12)

1. People aren't difficult, but their behaviors can be.

2. Choose from any of the 24 behaviors listed on page 10.

3. False—Heredity does play a role in the development of difficult behavior, but most difficult behaviors develop as people adapt to their life experiences.

Chapter Two (page 31)

1. a. Physical characteristics
    b. Mental characteristics
    c. Emotional characteristics

2. When our physical characteristics help us to be easily accepted and reinforce a positive self-image, we are more likely to relate positively to other people. But when our physical characteristics bring us rejection and personal dissatisfaction, we are more likely to relate negatively to people and exhibit negative behaviors.

3. a. Visual
    b. Auditory
    c. Emotional

4. False—A supervisor should never try to counsel an employee. Instead, the supervisor should refer the employee to a mental health professional.

5. a. Early childhood: The period during which most fears are developed.
    b. Late childhood: The period during which children learn to relate to others.
    c. Adolescence: The period during which children cope with hormonal changes.
    d. Early adulthood: The period during which young people learn to handle responsibility.

Chapter Three (page 42)

1. Heredity + Experience = Personality

2. Dominant—c. Very task-oriented and driven
   Extrovert—b. Makes decisions based on emotions
   Patient—a. Good at mediating conflict
   Conformist—d. Content to be alone

3. False—Each person has some unique blend of all four types, with one type being prevalent.

4. True

5. You can't change other people. You can only change environments and your own behavior to motivate others to change themselves.

Chapter Four (page 54)

1. c. Slow to take action.

2. True

3. False—Dominants prefer communication that emphasizes factual and logical summaries.

4. Confront Dominants about their actions and how they made you feel or the effect they had. Ask them to give more thought to how others will perceive and respond before they speak or take action. When problems are pointed out, they are usually sorry and apologize.

5. True

Chapter Five (page 67)

1. b. Enjoys repetitive tasks.

2. False—Extroverts need a lot of approval and affirmation from others, especially when they've been helpful.

3. False—Extroverts enjoy competition and don't mind losing.

4. When you must relay negative information that will affect an Extrovert's standing within a group, try to offer one or two ways for the Extrovert to save face, such as sharing the blame with yourself or some external situation.

5. True

Chapter Six (page 79)

1. a. Has difficulty listening.

2. False—Large amounts of information or stress can cause a Patient person to shut down.

3. Provide Patients with as much information as possible and time to absorb it.

4. False—Patient people often state their opinions indirectly.

5. Avoid problems before they start by treating all employees fairly. When problems do arise, negotiate to resolve them as quickly as possible.

Chapter Seven (page 90)

1. d. Unable to work with rules and authority.

2. True

3. False—Conformists strive for self-control and expect the same self-control in others.

4. Listen to what Conformists have to say. They always back up their opinions with facts and may have noticed potential problems others have overlooked.

5. False—Conformists enjoy competing against their own performance or environmental factors, but dislike direct competition against other people.

Chapter Eight (page 107)

1. Dishonesty in the workplace stems from an absence of values and the ability to justify immoral behavior.

2. Negativity or bitterness

3. Step 1: Coaching

   Step 2: Discipline

   Step 3: Termination

4. When confronting an employee about difficult behavior, a supervisor should focus on the observable behavior, not the employee's attitude or character.

5. Documentation allows you to trace the employee's progress in improving the behavior. Documentation can also help you legally defend discipline or termination procedures if they become necessary.